MONEY

UNDERSTANDING WEALTH IN GOD'S ECONOMY

Troy L. Peterson

MONEY
Understanding Wealth In God's Economy

Published By: 4 Rivers Publishing

ISBN 979-8-9899688-0-0

www.TroyLPeterson.com

Contents

Introduction

It is sad that many people don't understand finances. In our modern society, money is treated as if it's a secular object having nothing to do with your spiritual life. Actually, this could not be further from the truth. Money is more spiritual than most people have been taught to believe. In fact, money, whether in abundance or in lack, has more impact on your spiritual life than almost anything else on this earth.

Too often money is allowed to dictate choices in life. Every time you look to your bank account for confirmation, you are allowing money to tell you whether you can or cannot afford to do something. Every time you feel a prompting to give to charity or a ministry and your bank account tells you no, you are limiting your spiritual growth.

The misunderstanding that money is not spiritual has left many people, even believers, powerless and impotent. I used to look at money through this lens, as a common object I never had enough of. I used to think if I had more money, I would have less problems. I even believed money was the one and only solution to my problems.

Thankfully, God took me through my own financial crisis which forced me to see the spiritual impact behind and around money. As I began to understand the spiritual implications and applications of money and its importance in my daily life, I began to change my view and alter my approach and my attitude toward money.

For me, that crisis started in the middle of 2007, when a great tremor began in the financial kingdom, known as Wall Street. The first rumblings of that tremor actually began years earlier in the form of maximized credit cards and overwhelming debt, both private and corporate. When the time came and the ground burst open, many people were blindsided by the drastic and sudden change in the market. I was one of those people. I knew there was a shift coming, but I had failed to walk close enough with the Lord to have a clear understanding of what was in store. Therefore, when the market started tumbling, my financial empire and my net worth of millions quickly crumbled as well.

In a matter of months, I went from thinking I would be set for life, to suddenly wondering how I would make my next house payment. Suddenly, I found myself deep in debt and struggling to find money for groceries. The pain of that season led me to seek God for new understanding. I had enough spiritual sense to know heaven had all the answers if I was willing to seek and ask and tap into the power of the Holy Spirit to find them.

This book is the story of the truths God revealed to me through His merciful Holy Spirit during a tumultuous season. These are the truths He taught me about His financial kingdom. These same truths can put you on a path to the prosperity God has promised everyone who follows Him. I believe in this season, God is firmly establishing His economy, and those who walk according to the principles of God's Kingdom Economy will prosper. Those who do not will fall victim to the greatest economic upheaval we have seen in generations.

In early 2008, as I began seeking God after the financial loss I had suffered in the collapse of the markets, God spoke to me very clearly. He said, "I am establishing ***My*** economy."

He explained what we were beginning to witness. Our natural markets were starting to fall and were going to continue to fall. Later, the economy would appear to be in recovery, and it would improve for a short while. That could mean more businesses will pop up, and new buildings will start to appear, but only for a short while. Then it will drop once again, and become much, much worse.

Now is the time to grab hold of the truths I share throughout this book and enter into the Kingdom Economy of the Almighty God. Now is the time to establish His presence on this earth and be ready to provide answers for a world suffering from a failing economy. Now is the time for God's people to rise up. In the pages of this book you will gain an understanding of both the positive and the negative spiritual influences behind money. You will learn how to overcome the influences of the world and the devil on your finances and how to step into the prosperity God desires for you.

This book is not another prosperity message. Although I firmly believe God wants to prosper His people, there were many things the prosperity message left out. There are economic principles which will help you operate and prosper in a practical way. It's critical for the Body of Christ to grab hold of the true purpose of money and position it correctly in life. Believe me, the enemy will bring financial turmoil upon this nation and your family if he can. But I believe you can be prepared to overcome any financial adversity thrown at you.

This is not a prophetic prediction of another depression. Quite the contrary. I believe the economy will continue to flow as economies have throughout history. I believe this is the beginning of the largest transference of wealth to be seen in generations. It's time for the righteous to inherit the wealth of the wicked. It's time for God to demonstrate His power on this earth. For Him to do that, He needs His people to have the financial resources and knowledge necessary to reach the world. I believe this book is a step toward gaining the knowledge and resources to reach and CHANGE the world.

Troy L. Peterson

Chapter 1

What is Money?

Money! Man has made money to be the single most powerful force on this earth. Throughout history, men and women have done vast and varied things to obtain it. People have built businesses both large and small, while others have committed dishonest acts to gain wealth. Mankind has worked hard, but they have also lied, cheated, and even killed to get their hands on money.

> *No servant can serve two masters; for either he will hate the one and love the other, or else he will be loyal to the one and despise the other.* ***You cannot serve God and mammon.***
> *Luke 16:13 NKJV*

Jesus knew money could corrupt men, which is the issue He was addressing when He said, "You cannot serve God and mammon." Unfortunately, this statement has been perverted by the enemy and twisted into a lie which strips God's people of the ability to gain control over the power of money.

The fundamental perception has been twisted into the idea that money is bad and considered to be a taboo subject. One of the perversions is the ideology making poverty equal to holiness. This is due in part because some biblical translations today read: You cannot serve God and Money. This has fueled the misunderstanding which pits money itself in direct opposition to God. It waters down the truth of the Word and helps to convince believers that money is bad and to be avoided. It also provokes the belief that denying yourself money is more holy than being wealthy.

Have you ever wondered why people get upset when money is mentioned in Church? The foundational issue begins because the enemy knows if the people of God understand the potential of true wealth on this earth, they will become unstoppable. But as long as he can keep you blinded to your own financial legacy, the church is limited in its influence on the earth.

This battle over finances goes all the way back to the beginning. Money is a topic in the Bible from the start. The earliest mention of money or riches is in Genesis, Chapter 2 where God is describing the Garden of Eden. This is before the enemy began his campaign of lies and deceit which led to the eviction of man from the garden.

A river flowed from the land of Eden, watering the garden and then dividing into four branches. The first branch, called the Pishon, flowed around the entire land of Havilah, where gold is found. The gold of that land is exceptionally pure; aromatic resin and onyx stone are also found there. Genesis 2:10-12

This passage shows the importance God Himself placed on the riches of this earth. Notice how the *first* of the four rivers surrounds a land of gold. The name of the river, Pishon means increase, and the land of Havilah refers to a realm or kingdom. In the beginning when God and Man were in complete and right relationship on Earth and before man ever knew sin, money was present and worth mentioning. It was important enough, in fact, that it was listed as the *first* of the kingdoms that Adam reigned over from his heavenly position in the Garden of Eden.

A deeper look at the meaning of Havilah reveals even more. The proper name Havilah in the original Hebrew means circle. Most Hebrew words have double meanings, and this is no exception. The first meaning mentioned is realm or Kingdom, inferring that when you're in your proper position, you are reigning over your finances. The second meaning is a trap. The indication is, to get stuck within a never ending circle which seems to have no way out. An unhealthy understanding of reigning over your finances causes you to get stuck in a trap enslaving you to money.

A look at this passage in Genesis 2 shows the position the Body of Christ, the Church of the living God, is meant to occupy. Genesis 2 is a picture of the Spirit-filled Life and everything you can accomplish if you live in your proper position. The other rivers in this passage open up the picture to a broader place. The name of the second river is Gihon which winds around the entire land of Cush. The name of the third river is Tigris, and it runs along the east side of Asshur. And the fourth river is the Euphrates. There will be a more in-depth look at this later, but it is important to see the whole picture. The second river, Gihon means grace and Cush means darkness. In this place you have grace to cast out darkness. The third river Tigris means a sharp or rapid voice and it holds back the boundaries of Assyria. In this area you are given authority to speak deliverance over the captives. And the fourth river is the Euphrates which means to bear fruit. For the most part, the western church understands the need to cast out darkness, to set captives free and to bear fruit. The failure out of these four mandates is reigning over finances. Many believers are trapped in the circle of lies and deceit which come with being enslaved to money.

Jesus also declared the importance of your responsibility to reign over your finances when He said,

> *No servant can serve two masters; for either he will hate the one and love the other, or else he will be loyal to the one and despise the other.*
> ***You cannot serve God and mammon.***
> *Luke 16:13 NKJV*

In fact, Jesus spoke more about money and financial management than He did on any other subject. In searching the Bible, you will find the New Testament, which includes the ministries of Jesus and His Apostles, contains a little more than 200 verses on Faith, another 200 verses on salvation, and over 2,000 verses dealing with stewardship and accountability for your finances. Now ask yourself, if Jesus and the New Covenant in which we live, placed such a strong emphasis on finances, why is it so rarely spoken of in churches today?

The answer was given by Jesus himself. Look again at this passage of scripture in Luke:

> *No servant can serve two masters; for either he will hate the one and love the other, or else he will be loyal to the one and despise the other. You cannot serve God and mammon.*

You can see here, Jesus gives identity to the spirit which robs your power and destroys your inheritance. The spirit is mammon. Mammon is a spirit that has infiltrated the church, robbed spiritual authority and placed believers in bondage to their finances. As you saw in the earlier translation of this verse, the word mammon can be directly translated to money, but the indications are much deeper. This is where the enemy capitalizes on the confusion between money, and the love, worship, obsessive desire, and enslavement to money.

Jesus understood the power of this spirit and its influence, which is why so many scriptures throughout His ministry deal with finances. He wanted you to have the correct attitude toward finances so you could rule and reign over them. Jesus knew what very few accept today—the simple truth—if you do not control your money, your money will inevitably control you.

Let's look in Matthew.

Don't store up treasures here on earth, where moths eat them and rust destroys them, and where thieves break in and steal. Store your treasures in heaven, where moths and rust cannot destroy, and thieves do not break in and steal. Wherever your treasure is, there the desires of your heart will also be.
Matthew 6:19-21

This verse states you cannot rely on earthly treasures because they will eventually wear out or disappear. One of those treasures, held in high regard in society, is money. You may have the hope that more money will solve your problems. You give up your time to get more money, allowing your time to be eaten up. You likely use your money to buy more treasures, like cars, clothes, electronics, or the latest smartphone, all of which wear out and lose value in a very short time. This puts you in the constant trap of thinking you need more money to acquire more treasures. But if you begin to treasure heavenly things more than earthly things, you will begin to prosper with true riches that do not wear out. A great example of true riches is wisdom. The right kind of wisdom makes you irreplaceable in your job and gives you job security. And true wisdom always comes from heaven.

It is clearly stated here, if you put your faith in money, it will consume your heart. Simply put, if you treasure your finances, the spirit of mammon has control of your heart, not Christ. It's the influence of mammon which convinces you that happiness can be found in riches and in acquiring more stuff. The spirit of mammon is evident in the attitude currently imprinted on society and is put on display by many with the bumper sticker that reads, "He who dies with the most toys wins." The quest for more stuff turns into a quest for more money, which turns into viewing wealth as success, finally resulting in the worship of money. If you treasure your finances, you have made them your master. If money is your master, then you are for sale, and if you are for sale, the enemy will find your price. You have a responsibility before God to put your money in its proper place.

The proper view of money

Money is unimportant in and of itself. It is nothing more than a tool intended to be used to facilitate the fair exchange of goods and services. It is like a wrench. A wrench is a tool used to install or remove, tighten or loosen a nut or a bolt. A wrench can be used for other things too, like hammering a nail into a wall, but it is not very effective. The wrench was designed for a specific purpose. Its intended design enhances lives by improving your ability to securely fasten objects together and make them stronger and more stable. Think of how unsafe your car would be if the manufacturer did not use the proper wrench to tighten the bolts on your car. You could be driving your brand-new car and suddenly a door falls off, simply because it wasn't fastened with the proper tool.

Money is best used as it is intended, and when properly used, it brings great blessings. But when improperly used, it causes great harm.

Money is frequently used improperly because of misunderstandings surrounding the simple and basic truths regarding money. You need money to conduct your daily business here on earth, but it was never meant to have the relevance or power it has acquired in society. In fact, it only has relevance and power because we allow it.

I remember the day God began opening my eyes to this unseen spiritual realm of finances. I have never been the same since. In late 2007 when the Real Estate Market and the economy was collapsing around me, I found myself distraught from the financial pressures in my life. During the previous several years I had acquired a substantial net worth of several million, which had lured me into a false sense of security. My trust and my faith were in my wealth. I remember telling my wife in full confidence that we had nothing to worry about financially. I told her if anything were to happen, we could sell one of our properties and live off the proceeds for quite some time. Then came a reality check. Over a period of six months, I watched my net worth plummet below zero and my cash reserves blow away like dust. Suddenly, everything I had built up was collapsing around me.

In the blink of an eye wealth disappears, for it will sprout wings and fly away like an eagle. Proverbs 23:5

At this point of desperation, I cried out to God asking Him, why? I didn't understand why believers, who know all the scriptures promising prosperity, seem to lead the charge into bankruptcy court. His response to me was clear. He said, "Because my people are serving the wrong master." The master He was referring to is mammon. Mammon's influence on society and the economies of the world runs deep. I am going to expose his plans and influence in chapter four. Right now, I want to focus on developing a proper view of money, starting with the question, what is money?

We have established the fact that money is nothing more than a tool. And yet at the same time, it is so much more. In a way, money is similar to food. When you have enough of it, you don't think about it at all, but when you don't have it, you can't think of anything else. Perhaps that is why money is the primary competition on this earth for our hearts.

Believe me when I say, I understand the pressures money can bring. The truth is, finances affect absolutely every part of life. They affect your emotional health, your mental health and even your lifespan. In fact, study after study has confirmed the existence of a gradient linking health to wealth. An article in

Bloomberg titled 'More Proof That the Richer You Are, the Healthier You'll Be,' says "People who earn more are more likely to be healthier and live longer." On average, those on the top of the gradient enjoy healthier, longer lives than those in the middle, while those on the bottom of the economic scale tend to be the sickest and die the earliest.

Money matters. I like how Zig Ziglar put it when he spoke about money. Ziglar would say "Money is not everything, although, it is rather like oxygen." No doubt you can agree, money is important, and having money eases some of the stress in life. Even the Bible says, "Money answers all things" in Ecclesiastes 10:19. It is the need for money which has caused the elevation of money and gives it undeserving power over lives. The truth is, money is important, but it's not everything.

You may be asking why then, if even the Bible puts such an emphasis on money, does it seem so hard to obtain and cause so much worry? The answer is found within your own thoughts and feelings toward money. Take a minute, and carefully answer the questions below.

- What do you think about money?
- Do you fear money?
- Are you afraid there will not be enough money?
- Will money change you?
- Will it make you better or worse?

The way you think about money affects every aspect of your being. If you have good thoughts about money and how to make it work for you, then you will likely enjoy an increase of money in your life. However, if you have negative thoughts about money, it actually contributes to your lack of it. Unfortunately, you may not have been taught the right way to think and act concerning your money. The result of this lack of training is evident in modern society.

Consider what would happen if you selected 100 people today and gave each of them $10,000, then told them they could do whatever they wanted with it. Would any of them have money left after one year? According to Robert Kiyosaki, author of Rich Dad Poor Dad, 80 of those people would have $0 left. 16 would have around $10,300, (which is what you would earn if you put it in the bank and just earned interest on a savings account) and the remaining 4 people would have anywhere from $20,000 to $1,000,000. What makes those four people who multiplied their money different from the rest of the group? Their attitude concerning money is what sets them apart.

Consider this, of those 100 people in Mr. Kiyosaki's statistics;

- 80% are very good at subtraction.

- 16% understood some addition and were able to use that knowledge to earn interest.

- 4% knew how to multiply and make money work for them.

From these statistics, it is safe to assume what all 100 of those people think about money, but just thinking about money is not enough to be successful with money. If your thoughts about money were enough to gain wealth, then more than the 4% in this study would have attained financial freedom.

As you can see, even though money consumes the thoughts of almost every living adult, there is still an extreme amount of lack. Perhaps that is why, according to a study done by yahoo finance in May of 2023, about 78% of Americans have less than

$50,000 saved for retirement and will be forced to continue working to make ends meet. Even as early as July 2003 in an issue of Time Magazine, 95% of people between the ages of 55 and 64, were still working, and planning to get another job after they retired.

Here are some conclusions from this information:

- 96% of Americans will never achieve true financial independence.

- 4% of people will have the resources to live the way they want.

So what's the difference between the 96 percenters and the 4 percenters? It's definitely not the way they earn their money. Rather, it's **how** they think about money and what they do with it that makes the difference. Most people follow the old school of thought that tells us that all we need to do is go to school and get a good education. This allows you to get a good job with a good salary and live a good life. The problem with this thinking is that your entire well-being will be based on your job, limiting your ability to build a secure financial future.

You may think you need to live off the income coming from your job. Then, as conventional wisdom teaches, you can use a little extra money to start investing. That is *if* you ever have any extra money to invest.

For those who do find a little extra, they will usually start buying what are called paper investments, such as stocks, bonds, mutual funds, or annuities. Then maybe, if they get really advanced, they might buy some passive income vehicles such as rental real estate. But even then, most will use any income from that rental property to buy even more stuff.

PASSIVE INCOME

PAPER

JOB

All of this looks like an upside-down pyramid, a very unstable plan for a solid financial future. It puts the earned income from your job at the foundation with a focus on acquiring stuff first and investments later. This is not the best way to build financial security. Yet, this is exactly how 96% of today's population attempts to build their financial kingdom. The other 4% tend to do things differently. Many of them start out with a job, just like the rest of the population. But instead of trying to build a life first, they build their business. This is a principle found in Proverbs.

Do your planning and prepare your fields before building your house. Proverbs 24:27

So, the 4% who are financially successful use their income to invest in and buy passive income streams **first**. Then they add the paper investments like stocks, bonds or annuities mentioned earlier to those passive income streams. Then, just for fun, they may even still have a job. But it's a job they enjoy and want to do, which makes them different from the 96% who work their job because they have to.

The major difference between these two groups of people is the 96% see money as their source, and as a result use their lack of money as an excuse for their lack of success. The 4% who are successful tend to see money as a tool. They usually have a vision for their lives and a plan on how to use their money. They tend to assign their money to specific tasks, invest it in things that bring multiplication, watch and understand market cycles, and finally, plan to leave an inheritance. 96% of people worry about money, which brings lack. While 4% have a plan for their money and make a habit of putting it to work for them.

The contrast in these two groups of people is the outlook on their financial resources and the methods they plan to adopt. Successful people understand the outlook on money leads to your feelings about money. The way you feel leads to the actions you are willing to take with money to gain results. It is more than simply thinking about money, it's using money as the proper tool it was created to be.

Truthfully, most of the 4% started in the same place you did. They went to school, got a job and began to earn a paycheck. But this is where the paths separate. The 96% used their paychecks to begin to build a life, while the 4% went about preparing their fields. The 4% received the same breaks the 96% received. They took different actions, and therefore got different results.

You know, your success has nothing to do with how much money you make. Rather, it's what you do with your money that matters. If making a million dollars is all you need to feel successful, then accept you are already successful right now. Making $1 million is easy. In fact, most people make more than $2 million during their lifetime. The average household income across America in 2023 is $56,940. Over the course of the average 40 years of working, that adds up to $2,277,600. You probably never took the time to add it up. If you had, you would know you are already a millionaire. To be more successful you need to use your resources differently. But, if making a million is easy, then why isn't everyone wealthy? Here are three main reasons to explore:

1. Many simply don't think it's possible.

Most people are suffering from a lack of knowledge of how to properly steward their finances.

My people are being destroyed because they don't know me.
Hosea 4:6a

2. Many have unhealthy thought patterns which produce lack.

You might call this a poverty mentality. It is not a spirit, like mammon, but an unhealthy mindset filled with fear. It brings an expectation of lack and need. This will be one of the first things we address to expose an unhealthy view of money in the next chapter.

3. The influence of the spirit of mammon.

This is a demonic influence which runs rampant in society today. There are several chapters dedicated to exposing the lies from this influence and destroying its power in your life.

The next few chapters will be a deeper look at each one of these three reasons, concentrating on exposing lies and excuses from the enemy which hold you back and keep you struggling with your finances. There will be an exploration of the principles of stewardship found in the Bible. These are the principles God put in place to prosper you. Once you get hold of God's plan for your finances, you will begin to walk boldly with a clear understanding of His definition of prosperity.

When the schemes of the enemy are exposed, you will realize all the fear, confusion and hopelessness are plans doomed to failure. The goal is to help you walk into a place of freedom from fear and hope for your future.

First things first. There are some terms, mindsets and thought patterns to identify and address. You may find you have believed a half-truth or an untruth your whole life. You may also find you were taught some untrue things, even in church. Take the time to dig into the Scriptures for yourself and embrace the promises of God for the prosperity He has planned for you. Get ready for some radical changes.

Chapter 2

Breaking Free From Poverty

*Money is like food. When you have enough,
you don't think about it at all. But when you don't,
you can't think of anything else.*

What does money mean to you?

When I ask this question at my seminars, the answers are usually the same. Most people say money means freedom. When I ask what freedom means, they tell me if they had enough money, they would be free to do whatever they wanted to do. Perhaps this is one reason why so many people play the lottery, hoping to strike it rich and be able to do whatever they want. Unfortunately, history has proven most people who win the lottery are often worse off after winning the money than they were before. According to the National Endowment for Financial Education, 70% of lottery winners go bankrupt within a few years.

This kind of thinking is dangerous because it actually puts your bank account in control of your lifestyle. When this happens, one look at your bank balance decides what you can or cannot do. It also prompts thoughts of, "If I only had a little more money, then I would go on a mission trip or give to a charity." This kind of thinking makes money, or the lack of it, an excuse for failure to take action.

There are countless examples of people who found fame and fortune in their profession and suddenly found themselves with the kind of wealth most people only dream of making. These people fell into the trap of thinking a lot of money would be the answer to their problems. Unfortunately, just like many of those lottery winners, these people found no amount of money would be enough to satisfy them.

One of Hollywood's highest-paid actors, Nicolas Cage, at one time had homes all over the world, including a castle in Germany. In 2009, the IRS alleged Mr. Cage had failed to pay more than $6.2 million in federal income tax for the year 2007. He was not living a problem-free life.

MC Hammer is another example of a person who fell into this kind of thinking. MC Hammer is the artist who recorded the iconic song, "U Can't Touch This". At the peak of his fame in 1991, he had an annual income of more than 33 million dollars. Yet, in spite of this massive income, he filed for bankruptcy just a few years later in 1996.

Then there is Elton John. Along with his success, he developed an excessive spending average of about $1.2 million per month. That kind of casual, thoughtless spending caused him to declare bankruptcy.

David Cassidy rose to fame as a star of the Partridge Family TV Show in the 70's. After some health problems, a messy divorce and several DUI's, he declared bankruptcy in 2015 claiming more than $10 million in debts.

Mike Tyson, also known as Iron Mike, seemed unbeatable as a boxer. He was known for his powerful punch and was feared in the boxing arena. Over his career, he earned more than $400 million dollars, but due to poor financial decisions and a nasty divorce, he was forced to file for bankruptcy in 2007.

I personally faced the reality that more money was not the answer to my problems. Before the crash of the Real Estate market in 2008, I was living with the illusion I was set for life and could afford anything I wanted. I have already mentioned how my story ended. I also went broke and filed for bankruptcy. This whole experience sent me from 'set for life' to the challenge of providing for my family's basic needs. Before the crash, I thought I was the picture of success. I thought I had all the money I would ever need. But so did MC Hammer and Elton John. It was a shock when I realized we all had something in common. Just like them, I thought having more money meant I was successful. Nevertheless, I learned the hard way that money does not equal success.

Many people today view money as success. They often look at people who live in big houses or drive luxury cars and count them as successful simply because they appear to be wealthy. The sad truth behind this illusion is, many of those people are far from wealthy or successful. They are merely living a life filled with bigger payments than you are. They often live fractured lives, alienated from their family members, and often go home to an empty house, having no real fulfillment in life. Although they look successful, they hide the real pain of failures on the inside. That is not success. It is a lie from the enemy which serves to give only the appearance of success.

Several studies show the impact of financial stress on families. A recent CNBC News report reveals finances are the leading cause of stress in relationships today. The Examiner reports approximately 65% of couples argue about money on a regular basis, and further reveals the odds of a marriage ending in divorce are about 45%. Sadly, thinking money means success is a catalyst for problems.

Money was once my definition of success. I dreamed of the big house, the luxury car, the grand trips, and vacations to exotic places around the world. I actually took a few of those trips. But now I see success as something completely different. I have learned, success is no longer measured by the amount of dollars in my bank account. Instead, I measure my success by the number of people I can impact in a positive way, and having money means I can reach more people.

Not one single person has taken their wealth with them when they died. There are, however, great stories of people who left legacies of love behind because they touched lives. Jesus is the greatest example of a man who lived a life which continues to touch the hearts of people around the globe. He did it with love, not by building stockpiles of money.

Jesus said:

Seek the Kingdom of God above all else, and live righteously, and He will give you everything you need. Matthew 6:33

It is important to note here, Jesus was never concerned about money. Look at the story in Mark 6:30-44. This passage states a lot of people followed Jesus out into a *deserted* place which is interesting. A deserted place is a place without the basic needs required to survive. Specifically, there was no food to eat. Jesus told his disciples to feed them, but notice what they said to Him in verse 36: "Send them away so they may go and buy themselves bread."

Can you picture how calm Jesus was here? He knew He was about to give them a peek into the real economy of Heaven. Jesus was about to demonstrate how the true Kingdom economy has nothing to do with the amount of money in your account. Instead, it operates whenever someone steps into a place called faith.

To demonstrate to them how Faith worked in the Kingdom economy, Jesus said, "You give them something to eat." Do you think Jesus watched them with eager anticipation to see how they would react to His command? He is a great teacher, and He knew the best way to teach them the power of the Kingdom was to put them right smack in the middle of an impossible situation. One only God could solve. Can you imagine how they must have squirmed at this instruction?

They probably reasoned among themselves a little, then responded to him from a place of limited understanding. "Shall we go and buy two hundred denarii worth of bread and give them something to eat?" Notice how they seemed to focus first on their bank account. Somewhere during this process, they calculated how much food they would need and how much it might cost. Then they posed a very sarcastic question suggesting to Jesus even if they had the money, they could not buy enough food to feed this many people. Their focus was more on the lack of resources than on the abundant promise of God. In other words, they made the lack of money their excuse for not completing their purpose.

Jesus, however, had a different view. He not only saw the promise, but He also knew the provision of God. Jesus was focused on the Kingdom, and He chose to feed them from the abundant resources of the Kingdom economy instead of being limited by their lack of financial resources.

This was a miracle, and it does not happen every day. But when God has called you to do something, like feeding five thousand people in the middle of nowhere, He will provide the means for you to do it. For God to make provision, you must build your trust in Him. You need to have faith He will provide, and then you need to put some action to your faith.

Notice this story does not say bread and fish suddenly multiplied and they were able to feed everyone. It says Jesus took it, looked to heaven and blessed it. Then they started passing the bread and fish around to the people. Somewhere in between passing out the meal and taking up the leftovers, was the miracle. Of course, you can marvel at the miracle, as you should—everything God does is marvelous. But beyond labeling this a miracle, what does a closer look at the two different viewpoints reveal?

The first viewpoint is from the disciples. They see nothing but lack. Thinking money is what they need to solve their problem, they look at the bank account, determining there are not enough resources to do as Jesus asked. They make a sarcastic joke and seem to accept defeat. Their focus on the lack of money limits their ability to minister effectively to the needs of others. In fact, if they were in a church today, they would probably close their doors in the midst of this challenge. They would pray for God to either send them money or send someone else to help the people. They were ineffective because they focused on the lack, rather than trusting in God.

Jesus, on the other hand, was focused on the promise of God. He understood in a Kingdom economy there will always be enough to meet the needs before Him. He knew His ability to minister was not determined by a bank account but was determined by His Father in Heaven. He knew if God wanted to do something for the people, God would provide enough resources to accomplish the task. Jesus knew sharing the Love of God was more important than any amount of money in a bank account. For Jesus, success was fulfilling the Fathers will and touching the hearts of the people in a way which met their needs right where they were.

With this kind of viewpoint, you can see money does not bring freedom or success and therefore, having a lot of money is not a necessity for freedom or success in your life. Many people think money is going to bring them security or status. There's also the illusion money buys independence, or it can buy love and respect from your peers. But the sad reality is, money does not bring any of this. In fact, none of these things can actually be purchased with money. They come from within your own soul.

As discussed in Chapter 1, money is nothing more than a tool. Used properly, it can help position you in life with freedom, success, security and more. However, when used improperly, it becomes a cage to trap you. At one time in my life, I was trapped by a lack of money. I thought my only escape was to get more of it to gain a sense of freedom, success, and security. And yes, having a little extra money does give you a little more peace of mind, but it does not give you freedom.

Jesus said:

When someone has been given much, much will be required in return; and when someone has been entrusted with much, even more will be required. Luke 12:48b

I did not understand this concept until I had reached a point in life where my business was supporting my family's needs without any problems. It was the point where we could afford to spend extended time away from work without suffering the loss of income, worrying about our finances or how we would pay for travel. Our business supported us very well, and also supported many other families. Naturally, our payroll responsibilities had grown right along with the business providing for our financial needs and those of our employees' families. The success of our business was provision for those people who had made themselves loyal to the vision of our company. And the increased payroll was only one aspect. We also had to accept the responsibility for our increased customer service, and our increased inventory. There were greater amounts of assets in our care, and a greater exposure to many different liabilities. All because God had trusted us with more and granted us an increase in our finances.

With the growth of our business, we enjoyed an expanding income. I believe God wants expansion for all of us. He desires that we live in abundance, and increase. But with that abundance comes increased responsibility. Jesus said in the book of Luke, it is the Father's good pleasure to give you the Kingdom.

The increase of our business is a picture of the increased responsibility which came along with the increased amount of money flowing through our bank accounts. Our expanding payroll is a kind of responsibility that comes with increase. I know it's hard to think of this increase as a burden, especially if you're sitting in a position of lack. The truth is the more you are given the more you will be asked to do. Providing for employees is only one simple example of this very important truth.

No matter which position you are in right now, you must recognize whether you have too much or not enough, money viewed from the wrong perspective will cause problems.

- What do you think about money?
- Are you afraid there will not be enough?
- Will money change you for the better?
- Will money change you for the worse?

These questions were in chapter one, but I want you to understand how important it is to answer these questions honestly in your own heart. Before you can acquire more money, you must first deal with your thoughts about money. You must have the right perspective in your spirit concerning money before God can bless you physically with money. This is a very simple and basic truth:

For as he thinks in his heart, so is he. Proverbs 23:7 NKJV

This became evident to me years ago when my family and I lived in an apartment, and all three of my children were very young. Two of them had just entered school and the third was still at home. During this time, I was in a place of extreme lack. I would lay awake at night fearing I would not have enough money to meet our needs. I feared I would not be able to make my rent payment and keep the modest apartment my family called home. I was so focused on lack that everything I touched seemed to fall apart and loss became an absolute way of life. It was just as Job said:

What I always feared has happened to me. What I dreaded has come true. Job 3:25

Around this time, God began to show me a few truths from my own heart. He showed the more I focused on my lack, the more lack was part of my life. He said, whatever you sow, you will also reap. We often hear this in church, right about the time offering is taken. But when you think about it, and look very closely, you can see it has always applied. This is called the law of reciprocity.

According to the principle laid out in Proverbs 23:7, whatever you think in your heart is exactly what you will have in life. As I focused on my lack, all I got was more of it. To change, I had to find abundance and focus my thoughts there instead. I needed to give thanks to God for the things I had and focus on His provision. As I did, things began to change. Here it is again from Jesus:

For whatever is in your heart determines what you say. Matthew 12:34

Take a look at what's really being said here. Whenever you think about lack, lack is exactly what is happening in your heart. When you're lying awake, thinking about what you don't have, it becomes part of your heart. What becomes part of your heart soon becomes part of your speech. Then what becomes part of your speech manifests itself as part of your world. The simplest way to put this is, whatever you say is exactly what you will receive. If you are continually thinking about your lack, and talking about your lack, then what you will get in return is lack. Jesus went on to say:

A good person produces good things from the treasury of a good heart, and an evil person produces evil things from the treasury of an evil heart. Matthew 12:35

I think this passage is largely misunderstood. To really understand it, look at a different definition of evil. Evil can be considered anything contrary to God's will for your life. Or anything contrary to God's Word. When your words and thoughts are contrary to God's Word and His promises over your life, you are focused on evil. You will receive evil things because you are thinking, feeling, and speaking contrary to His Word. But if you can take your mind off lack and start to be thankful for and give praise and honor to God, you will begin to see and understand His abundance. You will become pure in heart and start to see good things.

I know this sounds simple, and perhaps even a little hokey, but let me assure you, as a child of God you have the same attributes as God. Genesis 1:27 says you were created in His likeness. If you go back and read Genesis 1, look at how God created the world. You will notice everything He created was spoken into existence. The chapter repeats, over and over, "God said it.... and it was so." Now consider this. God created the world by speaking, and we are created in the likeness of God. Then it stands to reason we also create by speaking. As a child made in the image of God, you have the power to speak 'life' into existence.

And now, dear brothers and sisters, one final thing.
Fix your thoughts on what is true, and honorable, and right,

and pure, and lovely, and admirable. Think about things that are excellent and worthy of praise. Philippians 4:8

If you want to change your circumstances, change the way you think. Then change the way you speak over your circumstances. Start now by thinking and speaking about all the good things in your life. Keep your eyes focused on them. Soon you will find more blessings and more opportunities coming your way.

Chapter 3

Symptoms of a Poverty Mindset

For as he thinks in his heart, so is he. Proverbs 23:7 NKJV

Have you answered the first question to your own satisfaction? What do you really think about money? If your thoughts about money are negative, it is likely your bank balance will be negative. If your thoughts are positive and based on the written word of God, then you will begin to see money as the tool it was designed to be. When you begin to see money for what it really is, your bank balance will become irrelevant, and you will be free to use money more generously. Generosity is exactly how God intended the tool of money to be used.

This chapter deals with what many people call the spirit of poverty, more often a poverty mindset or poverty mentality. There is no actual spirit of poverty. Although there are demonic forces who can influence you toward poverty, it is not an actual spirit creating poverty. Poverty is a condition of the mind. To better understand this, a definition for poverty is *a state of lack*. Throughout the politically correct culture today, poverty is used to describe the poor. But in the truest sense, the definition of poverty is simply a state of lack. If you are trapped in a place where you're constantly sweating and straining to meet your bills every month, you are experiencing lack. If you are always afraid there won't be enough food or money, then you are experiencing poverty. By definition, they are the same.

It is important to point out, life is composed of different earning seasons. There are seasons when you make a lot of money, and seasons when you make none. For my family, those seasons were quite extreme. While for others, the swings between high and low earning seasons may be more subtle.

Still, it is true no matter who you are, your status or profession, you will experience different economic seasons. Your earnings will go up and down in accordance with each season.

The season when your earnings go down should not be considered a state of poverty or lack. Rather, recognize the transitory state of a season. A transitory season of lack can be prolonged by allowing your mind to become hyper focused on the lack. Your focus can cause a continued manifestation of lack throughout seasons intended to be earning times. Perhaps this is what Jesus was referring to when He said:

Therefore take heed how you hear. For whoever has, to him more will be given; and whoever does not have, even what he seems to have will be taken from him."' Luke 8:18 NKJV

How do you stop being hyper focused on lack? It is not as hard as you may think. Start by renewing your mind.

Don't copy the behavior and customs of this world, but let God transform you into a new person by changing the way you think. Then you will learn to know God's will for you, which is good and pleasing and perfect. Romans 12:2

The world tells you to be stressed and worried about money, but God says His "grace is sufficient" (2 Corinthians 12:9), and He "will supply all of your needs according to His glorious riches" (Philippians 4:19). Breaking the mindset which causes poverty, requires renewing your mind and learning to build faith in the promises of God.

This may sound too simple but drilling deeper will expose the identifying symptoms of a poverty mindset. Be honest with yourself, if you detect any of these symptoms. Now is the time to repent and begin to renew your mind with the promises of

God. You want to be able to achieve all He has created you to do and be.

Poverty Symptom #1 - Lovers of Pleasure

The first symptom leading to poverty is being a lover of pleasure. It is arguably the number one symptom of a poverty mindset because society is 100% geared towards pleasure. Think about it. You are compelled to drive nice cars, live in high end homes, watch big TV screens, wear nice clothing and go on exotic vacations. Some people label it 'keeping up with the Joneses' syndrome. Pursuing pleasure to the detriment of your budget is the danger of this symptom. I have dreamed the dream of sitting on a white sandy beach in front of azure blue waters with a cool drink and an umbrella. Those dream trips are nice, but they have a place and a season.

Inviting poverty to be your friend can occur simply by putting a greater emphasis on pleasure than on prosperity. The pursuit of pleasure reaps the result of lack. Bloomberg reports as many as half of today's families do not have enough savings to take care of an unexpected minor emergency. This means something as simple as a flat tire could be a life-altering catastrophe for many families. This pursuit of pleasure is paramount in society today. It is part of the world's system of economy and causes you to sacrifice family for the appearance of pleasure.

Those who love pleasure become poor; those who love wine and luxury will never be rich. Proverbs 21:17

The word poor in this scripture has the same definition we are using for poverty. It is referring to a state of lack. In other words, to be poor is not having enough to meet the necessities of life. Recreation or pleasure in and of itself is not bad. I enjoyed my life and took wonderful vacations. I have driven nice cars and live in a nice home. But I have come to understand, those things cannot be the ultimate goal in order to enjoy true prosperity.

In the middle of the most difficult financial year of my life, I noticed my family seemed stretched too thin, and desperately needed a vacation. By this time, I had no clue where my house payment was going to come from. I had no job and what little income we had was not enough to cover our bills. But I had learned not to let my bank account control my life. I knew we all needed a break, and God would provide. After seeking the Lord for wisdom and direction, I found a state park on a white sandy beach—resembling a luxury beach on vacation brochures—and took my family camping.

Admittedly, this was not the most luxurious of vacations. There were plenty of bugs, lots of dirt, and what I would call roughing it, but we had so much fun. Even though this place lacked some of the basic comforts of a luxury vacation, my family and I had a great time. It was probably one of the least drama-filled vacations my family had ever taken. Having three daughters can make simply walking down the stairs a dramatic event. Cramming the three of them in a tiny room in a camper could have been a disaster. However, everyone was so grateful to get away and relax, that the drama turned out to be minimal. Thanks to the leadership of the Lord, this week-long vacation for 5 only cost $600.

When we returned, we found God had provided an opportunity for us to earn extra income. With this opportunity, our business received enough to cover a few months' worth of bills and keep us comfortably afloat. In spite of all the potentially negative circumstances, God made a way for us to cover all our bills and still have time together as a family. The vacation time caused us to grow and prosper as a family and drew us closer together. We were able to share with each other and work through a challenging time for all of us. After the trip we were closer as a family, closer to the Lord, plus we had increased in wisdom and were stronger in our faith. Our family acknowledged God was our only provider. We experienced real prosperity. A prosperous life is more important to God than a comfortable life. Seeking comfort and pleasure above other things will result in a state of lack.

Poverty Symptom #2 - Worry

Another symptom of a poverty mentality is the fear of lack or worry.

How many times have you found yourself lying awake at night worrying how you are going to pay your bills? I have had my share of sleepless, worry-filled nights. I understand financial stress. I lost my family's first home to foreclosure, I have disconnected my phone to stop the calls from bill collectors, and I have declared bankruptcy 3 times. I very intimately understand the stress of being unable to pay bills.

However, there is another truth to this. If you are lying awake at night worrying about your bills, you are not putting your faith in God. When you truly believe God will take care of you—in the same way a child believes his parents will take care of him—then you will be able to sleep at night. When you lay awake in worry, you have set your problems up to be bigger than God. You are dwelling on, focusing on and essentially worshiping your problems instead of God. This is a big victory for the enemy. Jesus gave us a very clear commandment then he asked a pointed question:

> ***That is why I tell you not to worry about everyday life****—whether you have enough food and drink, or enough clothes to wear. Isn't life more than food, and your body more than clothing? Look at the birds. They don't plant or harvest or store food in barns, for your heavenly Father feeds them.*

And aren't you far more valuable to him than they are? ***Can all your worries add a single moment to your life?***
Matthew 6:25-27

Jesus was speaking in response to people who had been worrying about the basic necessities of life. He was telling them that worrying would do absolutely nothing to add to their lives. Just a couple of verses earlier, Jesus is dealing with the thoughts and focus of the mind. He was illustrating the importance of your focus. If you are dwelling on lack rather than the One who can meet your need, then lack is what you will have. Look at verses 22 and 23 in which Jesus says:

Your eye is like a lamp that provides light for your body. When your eye is healthy, your whole body is filled with light. But when your eye is unhealthy, your whole body is filled with darkness. Matthew 6:22-23a

Take a look at exactly what He's saying here. Whatever you focus your eye on is what's going to manifest in your life. If you choose to look upon lack, which is darkness and contrary to the Word of God, then you will receive darkness. In fact, your whole body will be filled with darkness. But if you choose instead to look at the promises of God, you will be filled with the light of His Word. Then your whole body, your whole being, your whole life will be filled with light, and lack or darkness will have to flee.

Habakkuk 2:4 says, "the just shall live by Faith." Hebrews 11:6 says, "Without faith it is impossible to please God." I have come to understand that faith works, whether you believe it or not. You will always believe in something. You're either believing in a poverty mentality, and therefore, you will continue to experience lack. Or you're believing God will meet all your needs according to His glorious riches and He will produce abundance. Either way, you believe something. Either way, your faith is in action, and you are receiving exactly what you are believing in.

A key to overcoming a lifestyle of worry is to be thankful for what God has given you and focus your mind on your blessings. Turn your back on your lack. Start thanking God for the good things now, and He will begin to send more your way.

Poverty Symptom #3 - Collecting or Hoarding

Another symptom of a poverty mindset is hoarding or collecting. Now, to be clear, I am not referring to those manic individuals on the reality TV show called Hoarders. That program shows an extreme condition resulting from mental illness. Hoarding is not always in the form of overcrowded houses with no place to walk. It is also not generally in the form of an obsessive behavior where you cannot throw anything away. Hoarding or collecting can simply mean you are afraid to let something go in case you will want it later. Consequently, you collect things which do nothing more than take up space in your garage.

Hoarding can be as simple as saving plastic bags, or keeping all the extra nuts and bolts left from some ready-to-assemble furniture. It can be storing extra canned goods in the pantry, or overeating in an attempt to keep food from going to waste. I have to admit, the last one was me. I still have trouble leaving food on my plate and have been known to finish everyone else's plates at dinner. I am sure you can imagine how it affected my waistline. Perhaps one of the greatest examples of this in the Bible can be found in Exodus 16. In this passage, God provides for His people by causing manna to fall from Heaven each day. He gave instructions to not gather more than they needed for the day, but some of them tried to collect extra anyway.

But some of them didn't listen and kept some of it until morning. But by then it was full of maggots and had a terrible smell. Moses was very angry with them. Exodus 16:20

Moses was angry for a couple of reasons. The smallest reason was the people did not listen to or follow instructions. But the biggest reason was they did not trust God. Moses was angry when the people hoarded extra manna because they did not believe God would provide for them. Instead, they put their trust in the extra food they had collected. They took the task of provision away from God and put it on themselves. Whenever you hang on to excess, you are telling God you do not trust Him in a particular area of your life. You are expecting to be a better provider than He is. This is a side effect of symptom #2, Worry. It causes you to hold onto things you should otherwise be letting go.

How does this apply to money? When are you holding on to money, instead of believing God? You may be putting your trust in a storehouse God has not intended for you to have yet. It could be by collecting a little extra it is causing you to neglect the most important part of Kingdom economics—Giving.

It is important to say that I strongly support having some savings. It is a growing savings account that empowers us to build wealth. But often we cannot grow our savings because we are holding on with the wrong intentions, and that kind of holding results in loss.

Think about this picture. You grasp something of value in your hand. To hold it, you must clasp your fingers around it. To keep it, or collect it, you must hold it tightly and not let it go. While you are holding this thing of value in your clenched hand, how can you pick anything else up? Have you ever tried to put more into a hand which is already full? It doesn't work.

No doubt, you have heard money referred to as currency. Have you ever wondered why? Money is called currency because it constantly flows, like the current of a river. You work to earn your paycheck in order to pay your bills, buy food, and put gas in your car. Money flows from your employer, into your bank account, and then out again into the accounts of other merchants as you buy goods and services. Then it flows out of their accounts to pay for their employees, and to buy more materials to sell to you, and the money continues to flow in a never-ending, never-ceasing current. That's why it's called currency.

Continuing to relate money to the current of a river, what would happen to the river if you dammed it up? You'll have a big reservoir to play in for a while, maybe use your ski boat and have a lot of fun. But if you don't let the river flow, then soon the reservoir becomes stagnant and putrid. It then begins to rot and die. The fish and plants which once thrived in the river soon choke from lack of oxygen. Before long you have a body of water, but it's dead, with no life, and it can no longer feed you. By damming the water, you cause death. Likewise, by holding onto money or things you will reap the same results. Death.

A great example of this is my father. He kept the first dollar he ever earned. It was a source of pride for him, but eventually, the holding of money became destructive. As his life went on, his financial burdens grew. When he passed away, he was in debt and left a burden to his family. After his passing, my mother gave me a box of his things, one of which was his first dollar. For a while I kept it, framed it, and put it on the wall in my office to remember and honor my father. However, his financial destruction soon passed on to me. I entered a severe time of lack and was struggling to make ends meet. It was during this time God revealed a financial truth to me. The principle of first fruits. The first dollar my dad held onto was the first fruit of my family's heritage. Proverbs is full of financial wisdom, and this is one of the principles I grabbed onto.

Honor the Lord with your possessions, And with the firstfruits of all your increase; So your barns will be filled with plenty, And your vats will overflow with new wine. Proverbs 3:9-10 NKJV

With this newfound revelation, I knew to break free I had to let the dollar and what it represented go. So, I put it in the offering basket at church the following Sunday. I was returning the dollar to its natural flow in the river of the Kingdom. After that, the river opened up and abundance began to flow in my direction.

There is one who scatters, yet increases more; And there is one who withholds more than is right, But it leads to poverty. Proverbs 11:24

This principle from Proverbs is completely contrary to the world's economy which tells you to save and hold everything tightly in order to be wealthy. But the economy of the Kingdom tells you to be generous and give it away. You need to plant in many lands to reap abundant crops. Generosity leads to life. By the way, generosity is not 'giving everything away' but hearing the Lord about what to give, to whom and when. When you honestly examine yourself, you will know if collecting is hindering your trust in God. The solution is as simple as repenting and putting your trust back into the Kingdom.

Poverty Symptom #4 - Feeling Powerless

An inward sign or symptom of a poverty mindset is a feeling of powerlessness. It is the feeling of being trapped by your finances, putting money in control of your life instead of God.

When I grabbed hold of this truth, I decided my bank account would not control my lifestyle. I have never regretted it.

Imagine if the apostles in the Book of Acts had let their bank accounts dictate their lifestyles. How many lands would have been forsaken and how many people would have missed hearing the gospel? How many cities would have lost the great impact of the presence of God? The apostles were the first believers who chose to follow the Word of God instead of the balance in their bank account. And aren't you glad they did?

George Mueller was a man who died with only about $200 in his bank account. According to worldly standards, he was far less than wealthy, and was not considered to be successful. Yet, George did more for the orphans of his time than many people know about. History records during his life he cared for 10,024 orphans—food, shelter and clothing. Mr. Mueller was able to do this because he chose to believe God and have faith in the abundance of His Kingdom, not the lack in his personal bank account. The faith of men like George Mueller, who simply cried out to God whenever they had a need was astounding. Certainly, he made personal sacrifices to affect the lives of orphans, but he learned never to let his bank balance dictate the way he lived his life. He touched countless lives with the positive goodness of the Kingdom of God.

As a child of the Most High God, are you aware that all of heaven is on your side? When you align your heart with heaven, there are no boundaries.

Jesus said, "If? There are no 'ifs' among believers. Anything can happen." Mark 9:23 MSG

If you are feeling trapped, take a look at what you are focused on. If the answer is lack, get into the Word of God and begin to focus on His provision. God tells stories in the Bible to give real people with real problems something to relate to. When you see regular people in the Bible and how God helped them overcome difficulties, faith arises with His promises for your own life. One of my favorite stories of provision is the widow in 1 Kings 17:8-16. If anyone felt powerless in life, it was this woman. In the midst of what she thought was the end, God was setting her up for a huge blessing.

This story starts with the Lord speaking to Elijah and instructing him to go to Zarephath to find this woman. Isn't it interesting how God was already sending her abundant provision, yet all she could see was her lack. When Elijah arrived in Zarephath he found the widow at the end of her rope. She had given up and accepted her defeat.

But she said, "I swear by the Lord your God that I don't have a single piece of bread in the house. And I have only a handful of flour left in the jar and a little cooking oil in the bottom of the jug. I was just gathering a few sticks to cook this last meal, and then my son and I will die." 1 Kings 17:12

She was preparing her last meal because her focus was on her lack, which was not only killing her but also her son. Focusing on lack affects more than you alone. When you allow yourself to remain trapped and powerless, you are not only killing yourself, but you are also killing the generations who follow you. Fortunately for you AND the widow, God has a plan in motion in spite of the circumstances. The question for you is: How will you react when God shows up to work His mighty plan?

The widow had reached a place beyond her ability to care. She had given up. Feeling powerless and unable to solve her problems had stolen her vision. There was no fight left in her, which is exactly where God needed her to be for His mighty plan to work. Elijah asked her to make him a cake out of her measly portions, and she did. As a result, God commanded her bin of flour and her jar of oil not to run dry. If she had allowed herself to stay trapped and powerless, she would not have been able to share the last cake with Elijah. What if she had a hoarder's mentality and tried to keep it for herself? She would have stopped the flow of God's provision and starved along with her son.

We are powerless within ourselves. Accepting this fact, is actually the beginning of the season when God can move in our lives and our finances. Will you react as the widow did and share what you think is your last meal? Are you ready to see the windows of heaven open and pour out provision for you? Or will you allow powerlessness to overtake you and stop you from inviting God into your circumstances? It's your call.

Poverty Symptom #5 - Instant Gratification

The next symptom of a poverty mentality is instant gratification. This has been rampant in society for decades. On your last trip to the grocery store as you stood in line for the cashier, you were probably dazzled and tempted by trinkets, magazines and other items demanding your attention. Merchants call these impulse items. They are things you would not buy unless dangled like a carrot in front of you. What did you see on the impulse aisle? Tabloid headlines which are created with a curiosity factor, incentivizing you to buy their juicy gossip. You probably have a dozen things in your home picked up from the impulse aisle. It is a very strong marketing tactic. The impulse aisle is a form of instant gratification. It falls in the same family as a lover of pleasure. Impulse items are a way to feed your flesh and satisfy your desire for comfort. Psychologically, you convince yourself that stuff makes you happy, and therefore you are successful. You may not realize it, but those little three- and five-dollar trinkets on the impulse aisle at the grocery store can actually cost you thousands of dollars every year.

Along with this impulse buying, instant gratification has other forms. Perhaps the greatest example is fast food. It is amazing to think you don't have to get out of your car to put food in your face. Simply pull up to a window at any number of convenient drive-through locations and two minutes later you have your next meal. Any longer than two minutes for the food to arrive can cause a person to be hangry—the combination of hungry and angry. Why is that? Because it's not fast enough. It is not instantly gratifying enough.

What about the frustration you feel when you go to a store to buy something, and it is sold out? Or if you have to wait for a week or more for a special order. Few will wait even a week anymore. Instead, there are other stores that stock it so you can have it today. Even Amazon can offer same day delivery in many areas, feeding our need for instant gratification.

I have fallen into this trap before. I remember going to a Home Depot because I wanted to put an electric fireplace in my living room. It was advertised on sale, so I went to pick one up. However, when I got to the store they were sold out. They told me I would need to place an order and pick it up next week. I was not happy, and definitely felt I deserved some instant gratification. I insisted they call around to other stores and find one for me. Of course, I had to have it immediately. So, I loaded up the family, and we drove 30 miles across the city to pick it up.

The unfortunate part of this story is how upset my family was due to the added time in the car. They had to listen to me complain about the store throughout the slow-moving trek through traffic. I even yelled at my kids when they got hungry because the extra trip went past our dinner time. The real price of my need for instant gratification was paid in time and hurt feelings from my family. Fortunately for me, they loved and forgave me for my nasty attitude throughout the unnecessary afternoon. We moved on without any serious issues.

The worst form of instant gratification will cause you to buy things before you can afford them. The simplicity of purchases on a credit card has indebted society in epic proportions. Hooking yourself with payments for 18-24 months or more to take an item home today is far too easy. Credit Card debt is dangerously close to succumbing to the influence of the spirit of mammon, which will be covered in detail in a later chapter.

Poverty Symptom #6 - You are the Provider

This symptom is a lie perpetuated by the mindset of poverty. You are your own provider. This is not even logical if you think about it. If God is your Father, and you are His child, doesn't that make Him your provider? The same way you provide for your own children, doesn't your Heavenly Father also provide for you?

Look at the birds. They don't plant or harvest or store food in barns, for your heavenly Father feeds them. And aren't you far more valuable to him than they are? Matthew 6:26

Why is this one of the most difficult truths to absorb? Because it is so contrary to society today. You are taught to pull yourself up by your bootstraps and make your own way in the world. Although you have certain responsibilities to work for your provision, everything comes from God. Why is it difficult to accept your form of employment or business has been provided by God?

This became so clear to me during the last economic recession. Things were really bad for my family. We had lost millions, and I had no reliable source of income to provide for my family. I was definitely feeling the stress of lack. Before the economic bust, I had made a tremendous amount of money in real estate. As a result of my success, I had been a featured speaker at seminars across North America. It was the seminars and webinars I enjoyed the most. It was doing those things I missed even more than the money lost in the crash.

I had been invited to speak at those events because of my financial success. When the market crash took it all away, I feared I would never be invited to speak again. The thought of never doing a seminar or webinar again was very painful and I was faced with a choice. I could either accept that I no longer met this world's criteria of success, or I could cry out to God as my provider, asking Him to make a way for me. I chose to cry out to God. I remember very clearly how hard it was to pray that night. I was hurting from the loss of my professional status, as well as my finances. Still, I set my heart to trust in God. I sat alone in my room and prayed very quietly. I told Him how much I loved doing the webinars, teaching, and training, and how much I wanted to do those things again.

It was barely 24 hours later when my business phone rang. The phone line was all I had left of my former business, and it now rang into a room in my home. It was almost 10 PM which is far too late for a business call and definitely too late for me to answer it. Still, I was nearby when it rang, and I was compelled to pick it up. The call was from a man in the opposite corner of the country who represented a company I had never heard of. He explained he had been given my name earlier during the day. Now, here is where it gets wild. He said he was looking for a spokesperson to do training webinars for his company. There were several scheduled each week, and he wanted to hire me to do them.

This was the moment I came to know God as my provider. He showed me He would make a way to provide for my every need. And even better than just plain old provision, He showed me

He would make a way for me to do the thing I loved. After all, he is the one who gave me the ability to speak and teach. When I submitted myself to Him, He opened up the position and along with it the provision I needed at the time.

Remember the Lord your God. He is the one who gives you power to be successful. Deuteronomy 8:18a

Too often the mindset takes hold, making you your own provider. You can become stuck looking at your job as your only source. But if God is your provider, then you need to acknowledge He gave you that job as His means of provision for your life. Also, if He gave you the job, then God alone has the power to promote you or assign you to a new job. Of course, this also means God alone can determine how much you are paid for your job. It would be good, instead of cursing your job because you feel you're not receiving the recognition or credit you deserve, start giving thanks to God for your job. Start asking Him how you can do your job better.

I did this with the webinar training position. I prayed and asked God how I could become better, and then I applied the knowledge as He revealed it to me. Soon, I shifted away from the company who had initially called me and gradually moved up to other opportunities. Within two years of the late-night phone call, I was working with a well known real estate mogul with offices on Wall Street. I was teaching at live events and consulting with people from around the globe. All this success came about because I decided to trust God and seek Him as my provider.

Poverty Symptom #7 - Jealousy or Envy

Another major problem brought on by a poverty mindset is jealousy or envy. Everyone has felt it at one time or another. When somebody else gets a promotion you wanted, it is hard to be happy about it. Jealousy and envy are right there as you complain how it should have been you instead of them. There are also those times when a friend or family member stumbles into an extra-large blessing. For example, a close friend or loved one receives an inheritance, or finds a great deal on a car, and instead of being happy for them, you feel left out or as if they stole your blessing. And to top it off you get angry because it appeared easy for them, and you are still struggling to make ends meet. That feeling of jealousy, if left unchecked, will drive you deeper into poverty.

For wherever there is jealousy and selfish ambition, there you will find disorder and evil of every kind. James 3:16

Speaking of jealousy or envy let me simply say this: You cannot cast a curse and expect to get a blessing! Dictionary.com defines both jealousy and envy with very similar meanings.

- Jealousy: resentment against a rival, a person enjoying success or advantage, or against another's success or advantage itself.

- Envy: a feeling of discontent or covetousness with regard to another's advantage, success, possessions, etc.

Now let's compare those with the definition of judgment.

- Judgment: the forming of an opinion, estimate, notion, or conclusion, as from circumstances presented to the mind.

As you can see, both jealousy and envy start as an emotion, but end up becoming a state of mind. Left unchecked, an emotionally driven state of mind causes a person who feels envy to judge the one they are jealous or envious of. One great example of this is the story of Cain and Abel in Genesis 4. Cain was jealous or envious of his brother Abel. He felt God favored Abel more than himself. This was due to the fact that Abel made a pleasing and acceptable offering to the Lord, but Cain's offering did not please God and was therefore rejected.

Now imagine you had worked very hard on a project and hoped to please your boss, teacher, parent, spouse, or whoever. Yet in spite of how hard you worked, they accepted someone else's project over yours. Would you become angry? Cain presented an offering to God which was not accepted. There was much more going on with Cain's heart in this story, explaining why God did not accept his offering. But Cain did not care about his issues, he only wanted to be accepted and felt he deserved a blessing. He became irrationally angry because of envy toward his brother.

"Why are you so angry?" the Lord asked Cain.
"Why do you look so dejected?" Genesis 4:6

This story starts by pointing out Cain was jealous or envious of his brother, and his envy led to anger. Finally, the anger led Cain to kill his brother Abel. (Genesis 4:8) Cain's envy formed an opinion in his mind fueling a rage which led him to pass judgment on his brother. This scenario confirms how jealousy brings about every kind of evil (James 3:16).

Look again at how similar the definitions of jealousy and envy are to the definition of judgment. You can clearly see both jealousy and envy are forms of judgment. When you feel jealous or envious of someone and start to speak out against them, you are passing judgment. You are actually saying they do not deserve goodness, but you do. Judgment is not something you want to pass on to others. Jesus was straightforward about judgment.

'For you will be treated as you treat others. The standard you use in judging is the standard by which you will be judged.'
Matthew 7:2

Poverty Symptom #8 - Feeling like a Failure

Last on the list of symptoms from a poverty mentality is simply feeling like a failure. This symptom, just like many of the others we have looked at in this chapter, can have roots that are tied to the influence of the spirit of mammon, which we will plainly expose in the following chapters. This demon of mammon wants you to feel powerless. It wants you to have this feeling that you'll never amount to anything, you can't be successful in your job, you'll never achieve your dreams, you'll never be able to get out of debt, you'll never be good enough, or successful enough and on and on. These are lies coming straight from the pit of hell.

If you insist on living with a mindset of poverty, you will be trapped in a state of lack, unable to enter the promises of God's abundance. The choice is yours to make. So make the right choice now!

Today I have given you the choice between life and death, between blessings and curses. Now I call on heaven and earth to witness the choice you make. Oh, that you would choose life, so that you and your descendants might live!
Deuteronomy 30:19

God did not create you to be a failure. You were created for a purpose. Those who fail to live up to their purpose fall short because of a lack of faith. Their fear keeps them from reaching out beyond their perceived limitations. They let their bank balance dictate their lifestyle, and they never step out in faith to pursue the promise God has spoken to their heart.

The answer to this is simple: Open your Bible! Read it! As you pray, allow God to reveal what His word says about you! Receive it as the truth God made it to be and begin to speak truth over yourself and your finances.

So don't be afraid, little flock. For it gives your Father great happiness to give you the Kingdom. Luke 12:32

One of the main causes of a poverty mindset and all the accompanying symptoms is simply a lack of time in the Word. Getting to know and understand the promises of God is vital to living a life of purpose. A lack of time in prayer, communing in fellowship with the Holy Spirit, will keep you in a place of confusion. Take time to build a relationship with Jesus Christ and you will break free of the mindset causing poverty. You will find yourself beginning to understand and live in His abundance.

Chapter 4

What Is Mammon?

Strictly speaking, what exactly is mammon? Some well-meaning religious groups have defined mammon as money, thus representing all money as bad. This has caused confusion around money and wealth from a biblical perspective.

"He that is of the opinion that money will do everything will be suspected of doing everything for money." - Ben Franklin

In today's society, the influence of the spirit of mammon has caused us to put a great deal of emphasis on money. The perception mammon has created is the more money you have, the more successful you are. It is this opinion which drives us to measure a person's success by the type of car they drive or the house they live in. Have you caught yourself watching a nice new Tesla pass you on the street? Were you thinking how nice it would be if you were rich like the owner? What you cannot see is the size of payments being made on their nice new car.

A few years ago, I started a business which helped people get out of debt. One client I was consulting with had a strong desire to get out of debt, or so it seemed. What she really wanted was a solution to her perceived lack of money. She wanted to fill in the holes she felt were lacking in order to support her lifestyle. I remember the day I arrived at her house to assess her financial situation. We sat together and looked over her expenses while her husband carried on in the other room completely oblivious to our conversation. It was already clear she had more problems in her life than just her finances.

Her first problem was the lack of involvement by her spouse with the household finances. Their disunity directly resulted in overspending by both of them. The second problem was the amount of debt they had accumulated requiring more payments than they could afford. Clearly, her problem was not a lack of income as she had thought. It was actually overspending which had driven her and her husband to the brink of bankruptcy.

For example, the nice new Mercedes in the driveway was a major factor in their financial problems. It alone had a payment a little more than her home mortgage each month. (Yes her car cost more than her house). When I saw her car payment alone was so high, I suggested she make one simple adjustment and sell the car in exchange for a more affordable model. She and her husband could change their financial situation dramatically with one payment. However, she would not even entertain the idea. For her, the status represented by the Mercedes was far more important than being able to meet her monthly budget.

Her attitude and unwillingness to make this one change made her unteachable. She loved the pleasure of her luxury car so much she was willing to endanger her future to keep it. Thus, her situation was unavoidable. I told her the truth, and as a result, I did not gain her as a client. I can't say what happened to this couple. I don't know if their marriage survived, but I can say it had all the signs of a divorce in the making. I do know they lost the home they were living in. A little more than a year later, I drove by and saw the stickers in the window indicating the bank had foreclosed on the property. Maybe they were living in their overpriced status symbol of a car which she would not give up. Maybe she lost it too and was forced to give up everything in her quest to look successful. Unfortunately for some people, this is exactly what it takes to shake them into the reality of their situation.

Society has been sold a lie when it comes to success. You and I have been wrongly influenced into thinking success is about what you have, rather than who you are. This lie is the result of a plan hatched by the enemy of your soul. It is a lie ramped up over the last century with the express purpose of putting mankind into bondage to money and making mammon the master of your life. This is the same trap which keeps many people from achieving financial success today. If you find yourself trapped in these lies, your desire to learn the truth has already set you on a journey to freedom. It is truth which makes you free. Jesus said:

The one who faithfully manages the little he has been given will be promoted and trusted with greater responsibilities. But those who cheat with the little they have been given will not be considered trustworthy to receive more. If you have not handled the riches of this world with integrity, why should you be trusted with the eternal treasures of the spiritual world?
Luke 16:10-11 TPT

In this passage, it is clear that faithfulness and trustworthiness are essential. Chasing after money will cause you to be unfaithful with it, eventually resulting in lack. Instead of chasing after money as the solution to your troubles, begin to pursue the true riches of the Kingdom of God. Don't misunderstand my statement. Money is not bad—quite the contrary. I believe money is good, and God wants you to have plenty of it. What is bad is the amount of power you give money in your life. When money has too much power, it becomes the primary competitor with the Lordship of Jesus Christ in your life. That is why Jesus warned us so strongly over and over.

No servant can serve two masters; for either he will hate the one and love the other, or else he will be loyal to the one and despise the other. You cannot serve God and mammon.
Luke 16:13 NKJV

It is important to note the context Jesus was speaking from when He made the above statement. Jesus always took great care to consider who He was speaking to. He intentionally spoke to their customs and beliefs in words they would both recognize and understand. Jesus spoke with absolute intention. Every word was calculated in Heaven by the Father because Jesus spoke only what He heard the Father say. Speaking with calculated intent, Jesus had a direct reason for his choice of words. With this in mind, what did Jesus mean when He used the word mammon? To understand better, look at the original meaning of the word mammon. According to the Strong's Concordance, Strong's #3126, the word mammon is of Aramaic origin and was used to describe the personification of wealth. This means when Jesus used the word mammon, He was speaking of an Aramaic god of finance.

When Jesus made this comment to this group of people, He was giving them a direct reference to a spirit who had influence in their hearts. How does the context differ in our time? Well, it doesn't. Today, mammon is still a major influence in society. It is your job as a believer to stand against its influence, to take control over your money and break the influence of this demon with the power through the Holy Spirit.

If you do a Google search for images of mammon you will find all sorts of hideous images. Some were characters used in horror films, while others are from cultish games like dungeons and dragons. Most are simply ugly images people drew to depict their own vision of the spirit of mammon. Be aware. mammon's influence in society is a very real, serious problem. It has infiltrated the reaches of economies from the highest to the very lowest levels. Its agenda is to drive people into slavery and bondage to money. To make us broke. To create a society of slaves who will give their lives to the bondage and pain which mammon can bring. Simply speaking, mammon is responsible for much of the poverty we see today.

In order to break down and expose the plans mammon has used to infiltrate society there are some lies to identify. These lies reflect societal attitudes towards money and are damaging at their very core.

Lie #1 - It's my money!

This is a dangerous lie putting you in possession of something which has no eternal value. In fact, the only value money has is what you give it. If you did not value money, then it would just be a piece of paper.

Treading down this path reveals the lie. If it really is your money, then you should not need to give it to the grocery store, or the gas station, or your landlord or mortgage lender, or the electric company, or anyone else. In fact, if you called each one of them to say you were not going to give them any more of your money, they would likely do something rash and completely uncalled for, like turning off your electricity, or repossessing your car. It sounds absurd, but it proves the point.

The silver is mine, and the gold is mine, says the Lord of Heaven's Armies. Haggai 2:8

The first lie of mammon you can break by knowing this truth. It is not your money, it is the Lord's. Because it belongs to the Lord, you must be faithful with this thing called money, and according to the promise of Jesus, you will be blessed with true riches. Lesson number one is to be faithful with everything God has entrusted to you.

Lie #2 - Money measures my success

Society has been sucked into a false picture of success. The picture is of well dressed, pretty people who are relaxing with cocktails on the deck of their yacht. Or they are sitting on white sandy beaches, or jet-setting around the globe as if they did not have a care in the world. All of these images paint a skewed picture of success. These images portray expensive luxury items as the indicators of success. Because mammon appeals to human greed, it makes these expensive luxury items become the goal. Therefore, it drives you to spend your money building on the empty illusion of success. All the while trying to convince you that those extravagant expenses will finally make you happy. This could not be farther from the truth.

True success has nothing to do with the stuff in your driveway, but it is what mammon wants you to believe. Instead, true success is fulfilling the purpose of your calling here on earth. Finishing this race called life and entering into the joy of the Lord is true success. Your purpose is what He created you for.

Those who love pleasure become poor. Proverbs 21:17a

It is clearly mammon's agenda to convince you of an illusion of success. Don't become trapped in the bondage of a pleasure-seeking life which will enslave you into poverty.

Lie #3 - Money brings security and happiness

I used to believe having more money would bring me security and happiness. And yes, I admit having a little more money does help me take some pressures of life in stride. But more money is far from bringing the security and happiness mammon wants us to believe. Again, these are the words of Jesus.

When someone has been given much, much will be required in return; and when someone has been entrusted with much, even more will be required. Luke 12:48b

This puts a different twist on mammon's lie about more money bringing you happiness. While it may bring momentary happiness, the emphasis in this verse is on an increase in your level of responsibility.

My wife and I were married in 1994. We struggled financially in our early years, even filed for bankruptcy and lost our first home to foreclosure. But through all our financial stress our marriage stayed strong, and our relationship flourished. For us, those times of lack were not our real challenge. The real challenge came the first time we had more money than month left. Suddenly, we had a large amount of money, and we could afford to make all kinds of choices we had never made before. Because of those choices, our marriage became strained, and we faced some of the most difficult challenges in our relationship.

It was the extra money putting us in a place where we could afford to make independent decisions. We started to make those decisions from a selfish position. Those selfish choices began to drive a wedge into our relationship. It turned out to be the abundance of money which was taking away our happiness and tearing at the security of our marriage. We had to adjust our thinking and come back together. We needed to stand in agreement over how we would accept the responsibility of our own financial increase. For someone who is given much, much will be required.

Lie #4 - Money brings independence

What does it really mean to dream of independence? Is it dreaming about a life where you don't have to go to work? Is it a life where you don't feel like a slave to somebody else's vision, but you are free to fulfill your own purpose? Unfortunately, the lie mammon tells us is money will bring independence. So instead of seeking God to help fulfill your purpose, you begin to seek money.

And what do you benefit if you gain the whole world but lose your own soul? Is anything worth more than your soul?
Matthew 16:26

The truth is nothing you're doing outside of your purpose will ever be fulfilling. And fulfilling your purpose has nothing to do with money. When you look to money to bring independence, you're looking to money to give you what only God can deliver. That makes money your master, and that kind of master does not allow independence. Only the Lord can give you the kind of independence which allows you to freely pursue your passions and purpose in life.

Lie #5 - Money defines my purpose in life

This is probably one of the most direct lies. If you think money gives you purpose, it actually makes your only purpose getting more money. If that is the case, then you have made money into your master and reduced yourself to a common slave.

You cannot serve God and be enslaved to money.
Matthew 6:24

It amazes me how a modern, educated society can fall for such a blatant deception. Yet somehow, people have become convinced money brings all the things they are lacking. Society is convinced more money will make them happier. Or money alone will bring security and success, and somehow fulfill their dreams.

Through his cunning He shall cause deceit to prosper under his rule;... He shall destroy many in their prosperity.
Daniel 8:25a NKJV

Of course, mammon knows human nature and has played all of these lies through the ages. At first, those lies were subtle, but over the last couple of generations, they have become bolder than ever.

Chapter 5

Exposing Mammon's Plans

Over the last century, mammon has worked its way into society and the accompanying lies are generally accepted as fact. In the 18th century, a group of colonies began to arise in what was then known as the New World. Today, we call that place America. As men and women traveled to this place to pursue their dreams freely, they faced and overcame many challenges and hardships. Somehow, all the struggles and hardships were worth it to break free from the bondage of their old lives.

Even as this nation was being birthed, the forefathers recognized the schemes and plans of the enemy. They also recognized the influence of mammon. They knew if people were enslaved by their money, there would be no real liberty in this new world. John Adams, the second president of the United States, felt very strongly about maintaining certain liberties for the people. He understood the struggle this nation had just gone through to win its freedom and did not want to see it lost again. He was quoted as saying, "There are two ways to conquer and enslave the country. One is by the sword; the other is by debt."

Andrew Jackson, the seventh president of the United States, also recognized mammon's influence and worked very hard to keep it from infiltrating his government. He was the only US president to leave office with absolutely zero federal debt. What were these former US presidents concerned with? It was the influence and control mammon places on society. If the founding fathers worked diligently to keep the spirit of mammon from infiltrating society, then what happened? A quick look back at the last century shows how mammon planned to slowly take control of society.

As stated above, there was a time of zero federal debt in America when Andrew Jackson left office in 1837. It came with a problem, however. As part of his abolition of debt, he eliminated the central banking system. Although his intentions were good, his policies created some economic instability, which continued for a few decades after his death.

However, the instability did not stop economic growth from occurring in many of the cities throughout this young nation. Approaching the late 1800s and moving forward to the beginning of the 20th century, the nation enjoyed a great industrial revolution. Railroads started carrying goods and services to even the most remote settlements, bringing wealth and prosperity for all. With this economic growth and progress came opportunities both good and bad. Those who understood the economic system were able to manipulate it, and it was the manipulation which birthed a financial panic.

In the great panic of 1907, the stock market fell almost 50%. The following panic caused people to run on the banks and demand to withdraw their cash. As a result of the panic, many banks found they were strapped for cash and were forced to close their doors. It threatened to cause some very serious damage to the already fragile economy, very nearly collapsing it. Had it not been for a group of bankers who banded together to shore up the nation's finances, there could have been a financial disaster.

This was not the first financial crisis, and it wouldn't be the last, but it was one of the most serious. It had been caused by a stock manipulation scheme attempting to corner the market on copper. A few greedy people tied up a bunch of bank money and tried to manipulate the market, but it backfired. Since they were using borrowed money, the banks they borrowed from were also big losers, and the ripple effects caused the stock market to crash. It was a disaster which demanded answers and people looked to the government for those answers.

As a solution or possible prevention from this ever happening again, in 1913 President Woodrow Wilson signed the Federal Reserve into existence. This new central bank held the promise of stable financial markets to avoid the panic created by the banking crisis of 1907. The Fed, as it is called today, is a central bank with the task of creating and controlling our nation's money supply. It is not a branch of the government but is an independent entity which operates within the government. The Fed can make decisions on its own, without needing approval from any branch of the government.

This new Federal Reserve System quickly became more than just a plan for financial stability. It became a new system for generating control. Despite being signed into law by President Woodrow Wilson, even he had great reservations about its effectiveness. He actually had this to say, "A great industrial nation is controlled by its system of credit, completely controlled and dominated... no longer a government by free opinion... conviction and the voice of the majority, but a government by the opinion and duress of a small group of dominant men." The men he was referring to are the ones who now control the central banking system called the Federal Reserve.

In spite of the concerns of our nation's leader, we pressed on. We failed to understand what this new banking system meant for society. The nation was suddenly able to create money from debt. I know the concept sounds strange, but this is the boiled down version of how it works. The Federal Reserve has the ability to create money and circulate it into our markets, while at the same time, generating debt for society to repay. I don't want to bore you with a bunch of facts on how the US banking system works, but it is necessary to have a basic understanding of the concept. Here it is in layman's terms.

There have been two types of monetary systems used throughout history. The most recognized concept of money is called a commodity system, in which the value of a commodity like Gold or Silver sets the value of all currency. Gold and Silver are the most recognized commodities related to the value of money, but they are not the only ones. In the early days of the US, tobacco was a commodity which became currency. With that in mind, you can begin to understand how the commodity a society values becomes a standard for money in society. Hence, the commodity sets the value for the monetary system.

Today, we live with the second monetary system called "Fiat Money." Fiat money is a currency established as money by government law. This is why the words 'legal tender' are printed on dollar bills today. The global monetary system operates on fiat money. On one hand it is good because the value of money is established by a central bank, which creates a medium for regulating purchasing power and frees us from the challenges of a commodity based system. It leveled the field keeping the people who owned the commodities from having all the power to buy goods and services.

On the other hand, the value of fiat money is not tied to anything of real value like Gold or Silver. Instead, the value of money is based on the relationship between supply and demand. It could be said today, the value of money is based solely on faith. Not faith in God, but faith in the government and the value of its money. The markets and banks of today place value on money through trading in the markets. If the general perception of a country's government shows it is governing well, their money tends to have higher value. If it is perceived a country is being governed poorly, their money will be of lesser value.

An example of what can happen to fiat currency when people lose faith in a government was seen in Zimbabwe in 2006. The faith in the currency of Zimbabwe was lost, and with it, the value of their money quickly faded until it became almost totally worthless and was finally abandoned in 2009. If you Google the Zimbabwe currency, you will find images of people taking wheel barrels of cash to the market to buy a simple loaf of bread. In a brief effort to keep up with the rapid devaluing of its currency, the central bank of Zimbabwe even printed a 100 trillion-dollar bill, (which you can now buy on eBay for about three dollars). This was the largest denomination ever printed by a government, but it still wasn't large enough to keep faith in its money. Today Zimbabwe no longer prints its own currency. Instead, it uses the currency of the US dollar and the South African Rand.

Loss of faith is not the only problem with fiat currency. To make matters even more challenging, today's fiat monetary system actually creates money from debt. Yes, as crazy as it sounds, money is created from debt. Again, here is an explanation as simple as possible.

Banks today operate on a fractional reserve system which means they only need a fraction of the actual loan amount to be held in their accounts to make a loan. So, for a bank to make a loan of $10,000, they would not need to have the entire $10,000 held in their reserve accounts. In fact, they would only need about 10% of the amount. To make a $10,000 loan, the bank only needs to have $1,000 in actual cash reserves. With this fractional reserve system, banks of today can generate up to 9 times their actual cash in loans, literally creating money from debt.

It is obvious what happens to the banking system when people no longer make payments on their debt. There were warning signs of what could happen in 2008 when the banking system went into crisis. It was the lack of capital which caused the economy to stumble, drove unemployment sky high, and sent the markets crashing. In the end, many banks collapsed, and others were bought out being forced to sell off their assets to cover the cost of the debts not being paid.

Of course, these banks are regulated by the Fed. As stated earlier, it is the Federal Reserve which has the power to create and regulate money. As part of the responsibility to regulate, the Fed started a process called Quantitative Easing. This means they started buying the assets of the failing banks and markets. The only thing they never explained is where the Fed got the money to buy those assets.

It works like this. When you use your debit card, you must have money in your bank account to cover that transaction. But when the Federal Reserve makes a transaction, there is no bank deposit to cover it, it is creating money. The most accurate way to explain this is the Federal Reserve simply creates money by printing it, whenever it wants, and then loans it to the government, who spends it. This concept of money goes far beyond our Federal Reserve. It reaches into the banks, and from the banks, into households.

So, a bank generates money from deposits. Those deposits are typically made by people like you. You take money from your household, and deposit it into a bank, and the bank shows this money on its balance sheet as reserves. With those reserves, the bank can extend loans. As mentioned earlier, the bank can loan money in amounts greater than its actual reserves. This creates a supply of money greater than what is on hand. Consequently, credit-based accounting puts even more dollars on the street. But that's not where this ends. Here is a typical scenario.

Suzy is selling her car. Sam comes along to buy her car, but he does not have enough money, so Sam goes to the bank and takes out a loan for $10,000 to buy the car and gives the money to Suzy. Suzy then takes the money from the sale of her car and deposits it into her account at the bank. Now the bank can show even more money on its books, which of course, it uses to create even more loans. This new debt creates even more deposits, which can be used to generate even more money.

No matter how you look at it, with the current banking system, it is safe to say all dollars are backed by debt. Now every year enough new money must be loaned into existence to cover the interest on all the money borrowed last year. Economists like to call this growth, but the truth is, you cannot borrow yourself out of debt, and sooner or later this system of generating money will collapse upon itself, which is exactly what happened when the markets crashed in 2008.

But this is not a new concept. It happened during the Roaring 20's, during the first decade after forming the Federal Reserve Bank. This was the first generation experiencing newfound wealth created purely on debt. In the 1920's, personal debt soared like never before. People bought and financed all kinds of things, like cars, furniture, vacuum cleaners, washing machines, and household goods. They even used this newfound wealth created by debt to buy stock certificates, which led to an appearance of even more inflated wealth. But it was not real wealth because it was all created by debt. It was a clever plan devised by the spirit of mammon to trap people by enslaving them with their own money.

It was during this time, Henry Ford, founder of Ford Motor Company, was quoted as saying, "It is well that the people of the nation do not understand our banking and monetary system, for if they did, I believe there would be a revolution before tomorrow morning." But the revolution still came. Not as a revolt, but as a crash, today known as The Great Depression. God, in His wisdom, warned us against this.

Will not all these take up a proverb against him, And a taunting riddle against him, and say, 'Woe to him who increases What is not his—how long? And to him who loads himself with many pledges'? Will not your creditors rise up suddenly? Habakkuk 2:6-7a NKJV

The warning was ignored and as a result of many pledges, the nation plunged into the great depression. But this was not enough to keep mammon from pressing an agenda against society. As part of the plan to recover from the Great Depression, there were many new reforms and ideas introduced. Although many had good intentions, the end result was still the same. Mammon trapped people in bondage to their money.

In 1934, the 30-year mortgage was introduced. Suddenly, home ownership was very affordable, which was a good thing. However, since then, buyers have become reliant on bank loans for housing. Today, the focus is more on the size of the payment than on the size of the purchase. Before the introduction of the 30-year mortgage, almost 96% of people who owned their homes, owed nothing on them. Today, almost 96% of people will never pay them off.

The deception of mammon continued to deepen in 1946, when the first charge card was introduced. This enabled people to walk into department stores and make purchases without money. Of course, they had to pay off their charges at the end of the month, but this still caused an increase in spending and a decline in personal wealth. This new form of buying without money was slowly gaining popularity. In 1950, the Diner's Club card was introduced. In 1958, Bank America Card and

American Express came along. But it was still not enough, so in 1959 the revolving balance was introduced.

At first, people were reluctant to carry a balance on their credit cards. At the time, society simply did not believe in debt, but mammon had a solid plan. The plan was a sales pitch by the banks of the day which convinced people the finance charges were simply a means for consumers to conveniently manage their money. Unfortunately for us, mammon's plan worked and by 1966 Visa and Master Charge were commonly accepted at stores.

Today, personal debt is counted at well over $17 trillion. Here is a more personal perspective. The average family in the US spends approximately $9,000 more than it earns each year. This is possible because of credit cards! For many families, those once convenient charge cards have become pathways to ruin. I call them plastic mortgages since, in most cases, it would take anywhere from 30 to 40 years to pay off the balances making the minimum payments.

Mammon has not stopped there. The plan to indebt people has become so effective, it is heard and accepted every day. If you pay attention to commercials, you will find new cars are sold with affordable monthly payments, not the actual purchase price. Credit card offers come in the mail, regularly advertising the convenience of instant cash available. Subtly, in very small print, is the mention of fees and interest you will pay for this convenience. Because of mammon's efforts over the last hundred years, today's families are faced with more financial stress than ever. In fact, the average family today owes about $143,448. You are literally a slave to your money. You work more and more to make enough money to pay your bills, usually just barely getting by.

It is important to pause here and say I am not opposed to debt. In fact, when used wisely, debt can actually help you build wealth. But before making good debt part of the discussion, the bondage of bad debt needs to be broken. Generally, people think the majority of their money goes to pay taxes when in reality it goes to pay interest. According to the US Census Bureau, the average person contributes 42% of their income to interest. This poor use of debt eats away at your resources and stops you from investing to build real, lasting wealth. The misuse of debt keeps you trapped in a vicious cycle, like a hamster wheel. You are working yourself into a frenzy but getting nowhere.

This kind of financial bondage robs you of your dreams. It takes away your ability to effectively fulfill your God-given purpose in life. It is the same type of deceit Eve faced in the Garden of Eden when the serpent convinced her to eat the fruit. In Genesis 3:13, she said, "The serpent deceived me." The word *deceived* is the Hebrew word, *"naw-shaw,"* (Strong's # 5377) which means to put into debt. When the serpent deceived Eve, it caused her to take on a debt she never could repay. Today those lies are still causing damage, but the serpent does more than just deceive. It also bites.

> and they began to speak against God and Moses. So the Lord sent poisonous snakes among the people, and many were bitten and died. Numbers 21:5a-6

That word *bite* is the word *"naw-shak."* (Strongs # 5391) That is the same word the Bible uses to describe interest, specifically, the kind of interest that is charged on a loan.

> Do not charge interest on the loans you make to a fellow Israelite, whether you loan money, or food, or anything else. Deuteronomy 23:19

This word *interest* is the same Hebrew word *"naw-shak,"* found in Numbers which means to *bite*. In the Habakkuk 2:7 passage a more direct translation says your creditors will rise up suddenly and *bite* you. Again, the Bible warns you, the interest paid because of debt is like the bite of a snake.

It has been mammon's plan all along to entrap with debt. Debt has led to many financial troubles in homes, cities, states, and nations. But it's time to break off the plan and the influence of mammon. Fortunately, Jesus came and paid the price for your debts. With His work on the cross, He redeemed you and set you free from your bondage to sin and death. When you receive His gift and step into His grace and mercy, there is mercy for your finances, too. When you repent of your sins and let the Holy Spirit come in, He will wash you clean.

And the people of Israel did as Moses had instructed; they asked the Egyptians for clothing and articles of silver and gold. The Lord caused the Egyptians to look favorably on the Israelites, and they gave the Israelites whatever they asked for. So they stripped the Egyptians of their wealth! Exodus 12:35-36

That is incredible! These people had been in bondage for 400 years. As slaves, they were not paid for their work. They were actually in debt their entire lives. Their deliverance from slavery included stripping their captors of their wealth. They were delivered by the same God who has delivered you, and He likes to show off by taking care of His people.

In this passage, God delivered an enslaved people when they repented and called out for help. Not only did He deliver them from a life of slavery, but He also gave them enough Silver and Gold to leave Egypt with an abundance of wealth. In the same way God delivered Israel from their debts in Egypt, He will deliver you from your debts today! All you have to do is ask.

Before you can fully repent of the wrong influence in your life, you must also recognize a few other aspects of mammon's influence. It is important to understand mammon would not be able to put you into debt if the lies did not affect society in other ways.

Chapter 6

It has been said you live in a material world, and if you ever doubted how true the saying is, just take a look in the average American's garage. The accumulation of stuff is at epic levels these days.

"Mammon is the largest slaveholder in the world."
- Frederick Saunders

Although the exact numbers change depending on the amount of digital usage, the average person is barraged with anywhere from 400 to 4,000 ads each day. Each one of these advertisements is designed to sell you something which typically promises to make you healthier, wealthier, or sexier. Since those are desirable things, you end up buying more of those products or services than you need. It's this added buying which causes unnecessary financial stress in life. Financial stress is a fruit of mammon's influence. It is mammon's plan to trap you and hold you in bondage as a modern-day slave.

The previous chapter showed how mammon has infiltrated society, and how the serpent has moved into a position of control in the world's system. With this knowledge, you now have the power to break its influence and stop getting caught in the trap. Recognizing the symptoms of the influence of mammon is the beginning of becoming totally free. Take an honest, personal inventory and check your heart for any of these symptoms caused by the influence of the spirit of mammon.

1. Worry and anxiety over money

As discussed in Chapter 3, worrying over money is rooted in an unhealthy mindset. You can take the first step toward renewing your mind and changing the way you think. However, you must also acknowledge there is a spirit influencing your thoughts and driving you to worry. It is hard not to worry. It is one thing to tell yourself or others not to worry, but it is a completely different thing to actually stop. Perhaps, because worry is often coupled with emotion, and emotion fuels negative energy and this perpetuates worry. But, when it comes to money, the emotion behind the worry has a different influence. The influence is the spirit of mammon.

The serpent in the garden was able to deceive Eve by appealing to her emotions and attacking her identity. The snake called mammon does the same thing. It appeals to your emotions with an attack which triggers your sense of identity, causing you to ask, "Who are you if you can't spend money on something you want?" (whether you need it, or can't afford it, or both) The spirit only needs to entice you a few times, and before you know it, you've spent beyond your means. You are in debt. Once you are trapped in debt, it whispers negative thoughts into your ear feeding your stress and causing you to worry. The serpent deceived Eve by whispering into her ear. The enemy's power rests in lies. It whispers thoughts into your mind with the hope they will lead you toward negative action. God warned Cain about this exact thing when He asked Cain why he was angry.

Sin is crouching at the door, eager to control you. But you must subdue it and be its master. Genesis 4:7b

The thought which creeps into your head is what you must subdue. Sin begins with a thought you entertain rather than rebuke. Notice how God told Cain he should subdue it and be its master. You must rule over thoughts obviously not from God.

The snake who traps you into spending money you don't have, is the same snake whispering negative and fearful thoughts into your mind and causing you to worry. The result is sin. Worry and anxiety over money is the opposite of faith in God, therefore it is sin. To stop anxiety over money, you will need to fill your mind with the promises of God. Stop listening to the lies of mammon and start praying and giving thanks for the provision of God. Through prayer and the act of believing in God, you will find peace and be delivered from worry and anxiety over money.

Do not be anxious about anything, but in everything by prayer and supplication with thanksgiving let your requests be made known to God. And the peace of God, which surpasses all understanding, will guard your hearts and your minds in Christ Jesus.
Philippians 4:6-7

I remember feeling the stress of anxiety and worry over money. No matter how tired I was, whenever I tried to sleep the thoughts in my head grew louder. Soon my chest would start pounding, and I would find myself wide awake and filled with worry. I tried to fight it but could not seem to get past the stress of finances. Then I discovered the power of prayer and reading my Bible.

One night, when I felt anxious thoughts come at me, and the stress was building to a point of breaking. I grabbed my Bible and began to read. The stress immediately left me and suddenly I felt peace flood over me. I remember how shocked I was when it happened. There was no longer any doubt in me about the power of God to bring peace which surpasses all understanding. From then on, every time I feel anxious thoughts coming into my mind, I begin to pray and read my Bible. The Holy Spirit washes over me with the Word and I am delivered from the symptoms of worry. Spending time in prayer and the Word of God is a key to breaking the influence of mammon.

2. Money Mismanagement

Have you ever stopped to ask yourself where all your money went? It is very true, money goes places fast. It is, after all, called currency because like the current of water, money flows. As children of God, we are called to be stewards over everything He entrusts to us. This includes money. At the end of the day when you find yourself wondering where all of your money has gone, you must acknowledge you simply did not properly manage the resources God placed in your care.

One of the main causes of money mismanagement is a lack of vision. If you have no vision for your money, then you have no reason to watch over your money. It is part of mammon's plan to strip you of your vision. One of the primary tactics to shatter your vision is the fear there isn't enough money to meet your needs. Anxiety at this level strips you of your power and desire to plan for the future.

When people do not accept divine guidance (vision), they run wild. Proverbs 29:18a

Overcoming money mismanagement begins by making a plan for your money. Learning to track your income and expenses helps you know where it needs to go before you find yourself wondering where it all went.

Another way mammon can strip you of your vision is to tempt you with a nice treat, like a trip or an expensive night out with friends. Maybe your friends at work are talking about their Friday night plans, and before you know it, you're committed to going along. Very often this kind of thing happens at the same time your bills are due. I assure you, this is no coincidence. It is the voice of mammon whispering thoughts and temptations into your mind. Mammon wants to strip you of your chance to properly plan and prepare for the blessings God has in store for you.

It was Benjamin Franklin who once said, "If you fail to plan then you are planning to fail." This very powerful statement says the same thing as the scripture above. When you have no vision, plan or guidance for what you will do with your money, then there is nothing to restrain you from spending it foolishly.

Fortunately, there's a simple solution for this. It is called PLANNING. I use a basic computer program to track all of my income and expenses. This simple personal accounting program helps me to plan my bills and finances in a way which puts me in control. Anytime I find myself wondering where the money went, I simply look at the spending I've entered into my program. From this, I get an accurate accounting for every dime I've spent. Of course, this program also tracks all my bills. Every time I make a deposit, I can accurately see what I need to pay before I take any liberty to spend.

There are a lot of great options available for tracking your personal finances. There are downloadable programs you can use with a Smartphone app, giving you power and full access over your finances at any time. Choose the system which works best for you. It does not have to be anything fancy, and as you grow in your money managing skills you will grow into the programs best suited to you. The key here is, no matter what program you decide on, take the time to use it. It takes a small amount of discipline to enter your transactions, but it is the one thing which will put you in control of your spending. It also helps to see what bills you have coming up. With this knowledge, you now have a basic plan which empowers you to properly steward your money. You will be able to restrain your unnecessary spending, making sure you are faithful to take care of your obligations first.

Armed with the power of a simple money management program, you will know what obligations you have coming ahead. This knowledge will enable you to make a plan for what you need to do with your money. The more you practice working your plan, the easier it gets. Soon you will find you not only have a better idea of where your money is going, but you will also have a little more of it, simply because you stopped letting it flow without any restraint at all.

The master was full of praise. 'Well done, my good and faithful servant. You have been faithful in handling this small amount, so now I will give you many more responsibilities. Let's celebrate together! Matthew 25:21

This is what the Lord sees as faithfulness. When you meet your obligations first, as a faithful steward, you honor God. When you honor God with the little things, you open the door for Him to trust you with even more.

3. Consistent financial lack

Another symptom of mammon is using daily circumstances to draw your focus, which causes you to see your circumstances in a negative manner. This brings hopelessness and often overspending. It works like this: You get a flat tire on the way to work. You pull over and change it, wondering the whole time how you're going to afford to buy a new tire with all the other bills you have due. The flat tire causes you to be late for work. When you finally arrive at work, you learn your boss has been looking for you and left word for you to report to her office after lunch. This causes you to start imagining what kind of trouble you are in because you were late.

Now mammon wants you to be distracted and worried, and this is the perfect scenario. First, you are stressed over the cost of the new tire, then you are stressed over what kind of trouble you are in with your boss. Then, as you focus more energy on the negative circumstances of your day, you become distracted on the job. You make a series of small mistakes which increase your stress, and now the trap is set.

Soon comes the whispered idea, you need a break to get away from the stress of this very bad day. The whispers tell you to do something nice for yourself and the trap is sprung. The next thing you know, you are headed out to treat yourself to a nice lunch which will help you feel better about yourself. Unfortunately, the cost of your lunch puts a big hit on your bank account, and the cycle starts all over again. Only now instead of just wondering how you're going to pay for a new tire, you also have to figure out how to cover the cost of your expensive lunch and still pay the bills. This is the cycle of financial lack.

Notice how it all starts with a thought mammon plants in your mind? It builds on the unfortunate circumstance of the flat tire to draw your focus, and then keeps you focused on an increasingly bad day. The snake used those circumstances to distract you and say you deserve a treat to get away from it all. Once the plan takes root in your life, you are trapped in a rut of consistent financial lack, pushing you toward the goal of being broke! This appearance of lack creates more stress, which causes you to release control of your money and defeats the purpose of your life. If mammon can get you focused on the bad things around you, experiencing only negative things, you will feel hopeless and caught in the trap of lack.

The good news is you are already on the road to beating this symptom. You are dealing with the root of the issue when you turn to prayer and put your faith in God. As you take steps to be a better steward over your money, it will stop disappearing like steam from a kettle. But there is another key to eliminating this particular aspect of mammon's influence in your life. Learning to see the good in your circumstances, instead of focusing on the bad.

Stop looking at your lack. Stop listening to negative thoughts and stop focusing on negative circumstances. Instead, focus on what you have and give thanks for it. This is a basic principle of faith, and it works whether you know it or not. What you believe is what you will receive. If you're focused only on your lack, then you are probably saying things like, "there will never be enough," or "I just can't seem to get ahead." If this is you, then simply stop saying these things and start quoting the promises of God.

And this same God who takes care of me will supply all your needs from his glorious riches, which have been given to us in Christ Jesus. Philippians 4:19

In the story of the flat tire, you could start by giving thanks that you had a spare. Then give thanks that you weren't hurt, and you were able to get to work unharmed. Then instead of worrying about what your boss might want to meet about, start thinking of the good things which might come from an opportunity to meet with your boss. If you were in real trouble, it would not be your boss but someone from HR looking for you. The most important thing is to trust God. No matter how bad the circumstances may seem, if you choose faith, He will continue to supply all your needs just as He has promised.

4. The 'I can't afford it' mentality

Here is a question I ask at my seminars. What would you do if you had more money? The most popular answer is they would love to be able to give to charity. I usually follow up with a second question. What charity are you giving to now? The typical response is surprisingly common. I can't afford to give right now, which is why I want to make more money. This is exactly what mammon wants you to think. The mentality proposes the only way to afford the things you want is to get more money. The only way to be able to give to charity, is to get more money. The big flaw here is, there will never be enough money to satisfy the craving for money.

Those who love money will never have enough. How meaningless to think that wealth brings true happiness!
Ecclesiastes 5:10

This particular lie can be very damaging. It is the lie which puts your bank account in control of your lifestyle by whispering you don't have enough money to do what you should do. When God gives you a directive or vision, but you are listening to this lie, you look at your bank account and allow the balance to decide if you can obey or not. You are giving your bank account more influence on your life than God. This is the plan of mammon. There is nothing worse than letting your bank account control your lifestyle. If this is you, then it is time to rearrange your priorities.

When someone says they can't afford something, it is not that they can't afford it, but it simply is not on their list of priorities. The truth is, you will always find a way to afford the important things.

Many years ago, I was dating a young lady. Naturally, I wanted to impress her, and I made quite a few sacrifices to please her. There was one particular time I wanted to take her to a very nice dinner and a concert at an open-air theater downtown. Unfortunately, I didn't have a lot of extra money, so I chose to make some sacrifices in order to afford this night out. The sacrifice I chose was my electric bill. That's right. I decided because I wanted to take this young lady out, I could not afford to pay my electric bill. And yes, my electricity was cut off which meant no refrigerator, so I couldn't keep my groceries fresh. No air conditioner, so my home in the middle of the desert became unbearable. In fact, all sorts of calamities resulted from my decision not to pay the electric bill. I could afford to pay the electric bill, I simply chose not to. Other things had become more important to me at the time. The funny part is the relationship went nowhere. But the lesson I learned as a result has proved to be invaluable. No matter what it is I need in life, I can always afford what is important enough to me.

Another way this lie can be damaging is by distracting your heart away from the love of God. It causes you to be more focused on money than on God. Judas Iscariot is a Biblical example of someone who allowed an unhealthy relationship with money to come between himself and Jesus. It ultimately led him to betray the Son of God.

Read the story in John 12:1-8. In this story, Mary brought in a very expensive bottle of oil and poured it over Jesus' feet. This act caused Judas a few problems because he valued money more than the act of worship. Here is what Judas said.

That perfume was worth a year's wages. It should have been sold and the money given to the poor. John 12:5

Notice how Judas seemed to think they could not afford to pour out this oil. Instead, he focused on what he could charitably give if he had the money someone paid for this bottle of oil. Here is the danger of an 'I can't afford it' mentality. It will convince you that you don't have enough to give now and cause you to think that if you had more, then you could give! The lie always puts you first, and God's purpose for you second. Judas' relationship with money was only one of the issues he was dealing with.

Not that he cared for the poor—he was a thief, and since he was in charge of the disciples' money, he often stole some for himself. John 12:6

If Judas had not been so focused on obtaining more money, he could have seen the kindness in Mary's act of worship as she poured the oil over Jesus' feet. Instead, he thought it was more than he could afford to give, and by selling the oil 'they' would have more money to use elsewhere. Judas bought into mammon's lie and put the money box (the bank account) ahead of the love of God in his life.

Whenever you catch yourself saying you can't afford to give, you need to stop and ask yourself if you are putting your bank account ahead of God's plans for your life.

5. Impulse buying

Another symptom of mammon's influence is impulse buying. To be convinced a spur of the moment purchase will bring you joy, peace, and happiness. When in reality, they are more likely to bring you bondage to debt.

Impulse buying is defined as the buying of goods without planning to do so in advance. Often, this sudden impulse feels good for a moment, but later brings about buyer's remorse. There are several tricks mammon uses to encourage buying impulsively. One trick you will find easy to recognize is the desire to save. This desire can often cause you to buy more and spend more because of the perception you are getting more for less.

There is a common practice used in grocery stores particularly. When you check out at the register, they circle a line of the receipt showing how much you saved by shopping at their store today. In reality, you did not save $23 as the cashier said. You spent $115 on all the stuff you have in your cart. The appearance of savings is a trick to get you to spend more. If you feel good about spending (aka saving), you will spend more and the cycle of lack will continue.

Another trick to encourage impulse buying is to place a limited time on the offer. Naturally, because you hate to lose, you end up buying the product and taking it home. You are probably congratulating yourself for not missing out on a good deal. It is this loss aversion tactic which traps you into the dumbest things.

One day I was driving across a parking lot when a guy flagged me down. I stopped because I thought he needed help. He actually wanted to make me an offer I 'couldn't refuse'. That day, not wanting to miss out, I listened. The next thing I know I was driving home with a large box of stereo equipment in my car. I paid $500 and knew it had to be a good deal because the price on the box said the SRP (suggested retail price) was $2395. Later when I felt remorse, I Googled the product and found it to be complete junk. I had been scammed. I fell for one of mammon's tricks and got stuck with a very expensive lesson in impulse buying. Since then, I know to stop and think about my purchases. If it is a big purchase, I talk with my wife and pray about it before I decide. Taking a little extra time to make that decision gives me an edge on mammon's lies and puts me in control. There is always time to think and pray about your purchases. Living a life free from buyer's remorse will also increase your wealth.

I do realize most impulse buys are for smaller items, like the three-to-five-dollar trinkets at the checkout stand that we discussed earlier. Those small items can be even worse than getting stuck with a big item like I did. Mainly because you don't keep track of the amounts and those small items add up. According to a recent study done by Slickdeals, the average person spends $314 per month on impulse purchases which means a potential of $3,768/year in unplanned spending on small, mostly unnecessary trinkets. Imagine if you had saved and invested your $3,768 instead.

Wealth gained hastily will dwindle, but whoever gathers little by little will increase it. Proverbs 13:11 ESV

It is mammon's plan to make you spend all your dollars, but don't fall for the lies. Instead of small impulse purchases, take the money and add it to a savings or investment fund. You will be amazed how fast small amounts of money begin to grow.

6. Stinginess, fear of giving or tithing

I see this more frequently in people with financial trouble than you can imagine. Whenever someone comes to ask if I can help with their finances, the first question I ask is, are you tithing? Almost without fail, every person tells me they cannot afford to tithe. Oh yes, they want to, but they believe the lie saying they simply can't afford to give. Nothing could be farther from the truth! You cannot afford NOT to tithe.

The real truth is, there is no way you can ever out give God! Malachi challenges us to test God in this matter of Giving. The following passage promises if you give, God will open up such blessings there will not be enough room to store it all. God makes a way when you do the complete opposite of the lies of the enemy.

Bring all the tithes into the storehouse so there will be enough food in my Temple. If you do," says the Lord of Heaven's Armies, "I will open the windows of heaven for you. I will pour out a blessing so great you won't have enough room to take it in! Try it! Put me to the test! Malachi 3:10

I had a young man approach me after church one day. He was interested in attending an upcoming financial seminar and he had questions about his finances. I asked him about his giving. His response was fairly predictable. He told me he was not tithing or giving at all. His money was very tight, and he was deciding between groceries for his wife and newborn daughter, or tithing. He chose to buy groceries.

I said nothing but encouraged him to come to the weekend seminar which totally changed his mindset. He became determined to start tithing, resulting in changes to his finances almost immediately. Within 2 short weeks, he received an unexpected payment of about $3,000. He received a promotion at work he had been denied for more than 4 years. The promotion came with a pay increase which enabled him to quit his second job and spend more time at home with his family. The best part is, it hasn't stopped there. This couple has continued to prosper, and their ability to give above their tithe has also increased. The simple solution is choosing to believe and obey God with your finances. In doing so you can experience the reality of God's promise.

7. Greed, discontentment

Greed is more than a thought pattern or belief you will never have enough. Greed is a craving which is never satisfied, no matter how much you may already have. Mammon uses greed to convince you there must be more and drives you to get it.

In the story, *A Christmas Carol,* by Charles Dickens, you can see the effects of greed on the character of Ebenezer Scrooge. Scrooge not only made himself miserable, but he also made those around him miserable. Mr. Scrooge was fearful of lack and guilty of hoarding. His fear drove him to greed and because of his avarice, he didn't pay his clerk, Bob Cratchit a living wage. Bob could not afford proper medical care for his son,

Tiny Tim. He couldn't even afford a decent Christmas dinner for his family. But notice how the Cratchit family did not fall prey to mammon's lies. They were not worrying, or telling Tiny Tim they could not afford Christmas. They were happy, in spite of the appearance of lack. Scrooge, however, was miserable and lonely because of his fear of lack.

This severe difference in attitudes resulted in vastly different levels of peace and quality of life. Mr. Scrooge, who appeared wealthy, was actually empty, lonely and very miserable. The Cratchit family appeared to be in poverty, but actually had a wealth of joy and happiness which was contagious. At the end of the story, it was the Cratchits who joyfully shared with Mr. Scrooge, spreading their wealth of happiness to a lonely old man who had been set free from his lifetime of poverty.

Give freely and become more wealthy; be stingy and lose everything. Proverbs 11:24

I have seen many people chasing wealth and riches at the expense of their loved ones, much like Mr. Scrooge. Divorce and loneliness are the result and instead of finding wealth and riches, they are paying alimony and child support. They may have successful careers, but what is the value of a good career if you come home to an empty house?

8. Bondage to debt

A major focus so far has been the plan of mammon to trap you into bondage to debt. Take time to check your heart again on this one. Ask yourself if you believe the lie of small monthly payments, or if you're ready to start looking at the actual cost of a purchase.

The borrower is servant to the lender. Proverbs 22:7b

9. Exaggerated emphasis on money

It is valuable here to repeat the quote from Benjamin Franklin.

He that is of the opinion that money will do everything, will be suspected of doing everything for money.

It is amazing to see what some people will do for money. You can look at TV programs like Fear Factor, Survivor, The Challenge and Love Island, to see people pushing the limits of physical and emotional tolerance. Of course, it does not stop there. Some of these shows deliberately place people in compromising positions to push the boundaries of morality. On some shows, they face disgusting situations, swap partners in a relationship, and pull cruel pranks on their friends and family. And they do all this in exchange for money. CBS execs have stated people are willing to bend their morals when something is appealing, and no one sees them doing it.

Unfortunately, we don't have to turn on the TV to see examples of how people will sell themselves for money. A study done by the University of Utah found people were much more likely to behave unethically when they stood to gain financially. The study was broken into two groups. Both groups were asked to do the same thing, but one group was offered a financial reward while the other was not. Those offered the financial reward were more willing to make compromises than the group who was not. The study proves what J.P. Morgan once said, "Everyone has a price, you just have to find out what it is."

If you seek money more than you seek God, then money is actually your god. If money is your god, then you are for sale, and the enemy will find your price. It is mammon's plan to make you seek money. The plan is to get you to believe all your problems can be solved if you get more money. This lie drives many people to compromise their values and betray their souls. Jesus gave a warning in Matthew.

And what do you benefit if you gain the whole world but lose your own soul? Is anything worth more than your soul? Matthew 16:26

You were bought and paid for by the Blood of Jesus Christ. He came and gave His life so you and I would live, and live more abundantly. (John 10:10). Don't allow yourself to be sold through mammon's lies.

If you recognize any of these symptoms in your finances, then it's time to make a change. Fortunately, you serve a God who is filled with mercy and grace. He is a God who loves to show off His goodness, and he is ready to show off for you today.

Then you will destroy all your silver idols and your precious gold images. You will throw them out like filthy rags, saying to them, "Good riddance!" Then the Lord will bless you with rain at planting time. There will be wonderful harvests and plenty of pastureland for your livestock. Isaiah 30:22-23

It really is simple. Repent now before God and confess the deception and influence mammon has had in your life. Then renounce the influence, decide to stop pursuing money, riches, and wealth, and begin to pursue God. In the name of Jesus, our Lord and Savior, God will forgive you and release His abundance upon you.

But blessed are those who trust in the Lord and have made the Lord their hope and confidence. They are like trees planted along a riverbank, with roots that reach deep into the water. Jeremiah 17:7-8a

Chapter 7

Your Identity Changes Everything

It was the summer of 1973, and I had just finished third grade. I was moving with my family from the desert of California to the mountains of Arizona. It was an exciting time since my dad was opening a new business and there was the promise of great things ahead for our whole family. Although I was more excited about leaving tumbleweeds behind and moving toward rocks for climbing and pine trees to play around.

I remember the day my family arrived at our new home in the mountains. When we got out of the car, we saw the little house was surrounded by huge pine trees and moss covered rocks. For a young boy fresh out of third grade, it seemed like heaven. In fact, I remember that day as one of the happiest days of my childhood. The little house in the middle of the woods only had two bedrooms and one bathroom which made it a little crowded for my brother, sister, mom, dad, and me, but we managed. The most important thing was we were together, and I had woods just outside the house to play in.

We didn't live in the little house very long. Soon my dad's business had grown and was making enough money to have a new, much bigger house built. It had three bedrooms and two bathrooms, and even a two-car garage. Plus, for added fun, we had an unfinished basement where my brother and I could crawl around under the house and get into all kinds of dirt. There were still woods out back which made me very happy.

Everything seemed pretty good with our new life in the mountains. I hardly even noticed my dad wasn't home much. It seemed normal he would need to work late, and I didn't think twice about the weekend trips my siblings and I took alone with our mom. I knew my dad was busy, and I learned to appreciate the times he took off to go with the family on camping trips or picnic outings to the lake. My favorites were the fishing trips we used to take. Those trips were some of the rare times I spent with my dad as I was growing up. I knew he was busy and couldn't attend my school events, so I learned to treasure the times we went to the lake with our fishing rods, slowly passing the day away. Those were the few special times we had.

Over the years I developed an interest in the speech and debate team. I was scheduled for a lot of school events, I gave presentations at big functions, and I was involved in school plays. As much fun as it was, I would've given anything to have my dad attend at least one of my events. But he was too busy with work and couldn't make it. I do remember one time hanging out with my dad, watching my brother play football. We cheered when my brother's team took the field and ate hotdogs while we watched them play. I can't even tell you if my brother's team won or lost the game, but it was a special day. The only thing I cared about was hanging out with my dad. It was something I didn't get to do very often.

My mom and dad divorced shortly after I turned 13. I moved with my mom back to the deserts of California where we could be close to my grandma and grandpa. My mom needed the support of her family while my dad stayed behind in Arizona. I wanted so badly to stay with my dad, but it was not an option. After living in California for about six months, I went back to visit my dad. You can't believe how excited I was to see him. I was a little shocked to arrive and find out I had a stepmom and a stepsister. I didn't really care much, as long as I got to see my dad. Unfortunately, my visit was cut short when he sent me home early. My dad's new family felt disrupted by my presence.

For the next several years I went back and forth between my mom and my dad's house. I was continually striving for my father's acceptance without any success. I began to believe that although I was his oldest son, I was also his biggest disappointment.

One day about the time I should have graduated, my dad called to say he was passing through town and could I meet him for lunch. Naturally, I was excited and couldn't wait to see him. When he came through town, he stopped on the opposite side of the city from where I lived and asked me to meet him in the parking lot of a fast-food place. I didn't have any transportation at that time, so I walked a couple of hours across town to make sure I didn't miss him. When I got there, he slid open the side door of his van to show me a small Honda motorcycle he'd purchased. He pointed to it with a big smile and said, "Look what I just got for your brother, do you think he'll like it?" I was crushed. Just a couple of weeks before, Dad had told me about a motorcycle he had found and asked me if I needed transportation. Naturally, when I first saw the motorcycle, I thought it had been for me. I'm sure you can imagine how I felt to learn it was going to be another toy he offered to my brother. As I mentioned earlier, my dad never attended my academic events, but he found time for my brother's games, so I should not have been surprised that this motorbike would go to my brother too. This became the last straw for me. It was at this moment I finally accepted that I would never earn my dad's approval and I would not get anything from him.

Those years of constantly looking for, but never getting my dad's approval, created a negative self-image for me. I told myself I was not worthy of a father's love, support, and acceptance. Therefore, I was not worthy of success. You may be able to identify with similar struggles. Although your story may look different from mine, you very likely have pain from your past which will affect your future more than you think. I was in my late 30's, and raising kids of my own when I began to realize I was still a little boy looking for my daddy's approval. Because of the painful relationship with my dad, I had developed the belief I was not worthy of success. Inside I believed I was destined to constantly look for approval I did not deserve. I was stuck in a cycle of unbelief.

You may be wondering what this story has to do with finances. It has absolutely everything to do with finances! Success is more than an outward manifestation of wealth. True prosperity comes from the inside. It's so important to develop a proper view of yourself and learn to see yourself the way your Heavenly Father sees you. If you feel unworthy of acceptance, or undeserving of success, you will be your own roadblock to achievement. When you feel unworthy, you block God's ability to bless you. You simply can't receive the goodness He intends to pour out on you.

For me, the relationship I had with my dad set the parameters for the relationship I had with my Heavenly Father. If I could not count on my dad to support me in the things I achieved, then how could I possibly understand the love and support of my Heavenly Father? How could I expect Him to give me what I had never known? Thankfully, God has a different plan.

So don't be afraid, little flock. For it gives your Father great happiness to give you the Kingdom. Luke 12:32

This was a new concept to me. I had to re-learn the Father's love and accept His grace over my life. I needed a renewing of my mind to allow the Word and the true love of God to penetrate my soul and govern my life. It was a Heavenly renewal which eventually brought great transformation in my life and invited prosperity in ways I could hardly imagine. I had never known the boundless love of my Heavenly Father.

The Lord will withhold no good thing from those who do what is right. Psalms 84:11b

Accepting His love is the first Key to prosperity in this natural world. Your entire sphere of influence will be conditioned by your level of acceptance of the Love of God.

Unfortunately, the enemy has done a great job of tearing down the support of family in a myriad of ways. Divorce is accepted as commonplace. Children from divided homes often end up living with a step-parent instead of their birth parents. Parents drag their children through second and sometimes even third divorces. Imagine the identity crisis this causes. Tearing apart the family also tears apart finances. Single parents who work multiple jobs are barely making it in today's economy.

Beyond the finance issue is the absence of a father in more homes today than a generation ago. According to a 2021 Census Bureau Report, there are 18.4 million kids growing up in a home without a father. The same study says households without a father are 4 times more likely to live below the poverty line. The National Center for Fathering adds that 72.2% of the US population sees fatherlessness as the most significant social problem today. Not only does this tear at the hearts of children, but it tears at finances in more ways than just the cost of divorce and separation. It robs people of their identity. This emphasizes the importance of a father's love, but even more important is the love of our Heavenly Father.

Biblically, a father's role is to provide for the family, but not just materially. In today's society, provision is equated with money alone. It is heartbreaking when well-meaning fathers and mothers give up precious time with their kids to make extra money, all in the name of provision. A father's real provision is three-fold. First, a father provides security. For a kid, the security of knowing a father's love and acceptance is life changing. They are able to witness unconditional love in action.

This was the hardest for me to learn. I felt ignored and abandoned by my natural father which made it hard to accept my Heavenly father. Thankfully, I reached out in faith and made the conscious decision to trust Him. I drew near to Him hoping He would honor His word in James 4:8 and draw near to me. One evening as I was reading my Bible and praying, the Lord spoke to me in an electrifying way and made His love and acceptance of me more real than I could ever explain. In Joshua 1:9 He said to be strong and courageous! Do not be discouraged or dismayed for the Lord your God is with you wherever you go. I read that passage and felt the electric presence of the Holy Spirit wrapped around me. His undeniable presence made His love real for me that day. I also saw in Deuteronomy 31: 8 where the Lord said He will always go before me and be with me and He will never leave or forsake me.

Looking back across the many challenges I've faced since then, I can say without a doubt, my Heavenly Father has held true to His Word. He has never left me. He has always been with me. He has held me up in the hard times and celebrated me in good times. I no longer question the love and acceptance of my Father. I am no longer a lost little boy hopelessly looking for his father's approval which will never come. My God has shown me I have His approval and I have His promise to always be with me.

The second thing a father provides is purpose. When a father steps into his true role as provider, he will help his children find the purpose and destiny they were created to fulfill. It's much easier to find your purpose when you fully accept and receive the love of your Father. If you truly love Him, you will spend time with Him. As you read His Word, He will unveil the purpose He has for you. In your purpose you will find fullness of joy and your life will become more than you ever imagined it could be.

Finally, a father provides identity. This is greatly missed in society today. If more people knew their identity in Christ, they would not be so easily swayed by the latest fads promising success. They would not be so eager to seek the approval of others, and they would be confident in who they were created to be. Identity is often what you are seeking when you chase after riches. Identity in Christ is what combats the lie saying more money will bring the desired security you never received.

The identity you crave can only come from your Heavenly Father. Only through the unconditional love He offers can you find the strength to recover from hard times. Only in the purpose He places in your heart will you gain the confidence to keep moving forward. Only the Identity He has created for you will bring success. I was robbed of my identity through the neglect of my own father. It was not until I finally grasped the truth of the love and acceptance of my Heavenly Father that I was able to step into my true identity, pursuing the calling He placed on my life.

What if you have lived your whole life with thoughts of insecurity and doubt about who you are? How do you begin to change the way you think and believe? It is simple. Find out exactly what your Heavenly Father says about you. Accept it. Pray and speak His Word over yourself—hearing yourself say it with your own words—and before you know it, you will begin to believe it's true. It is not difficult to accept God's word as truth. Even those who question the Bible agree to the facts contained within its pages. If you agree the Bible is the undeniable truth of God, then every word written in it is truth for your life.

What exactly does God's Word say about you? There are promises God has spoken throughout His written word. Begin to speak them out loud and confess them over your life. You can start right now by renewing your mind and accepting the identity your Heavenly Father has given you since before the day you were born. After all, it was God who began all things, and it was God who planned for you from the start of time. There are many scriptures that show that it was God who formed you before you were born.

Thus says the Lord who made you And formed you from the womb, who will help you Isaiah 44:2a NKJV

You made all the delicate, inner parts of my body and knit me together in my mother's womb. ' Psalms 139:13

I knew you before I formed you in your mother's womb. Before you were born I set you apart and appointed you as my prophet to the nations. Jeremiah 1:5

God has intended for you to be here on this earth, reading this book right now. He does not select just a few special people, but His Word is for all. His Word says He does not show partiality.

For God does not show favoritism. Romans 2:11

God does not play favorites. He formed you, and He planned for you, and He did it before you ever existed on this earth. Therefore, it is safe to say God has a plan for you, and all you need to do is ask Him to reveal it to you. It is the enemy who has lied, said you're not worthy, robbed your identity and kept you from fulfilling the purpose God intended for you. The first step in breaking the lies and moving forward to achieve the success you've dreamed of is accepting the love of your Heavenly Father, God.

Your identity affects how you see yourself, what you think you are capable of and what you deserve. In my own life, I struggled and clawed and fought and kicked and screamed, all in vain because I felt unworthy of success. No matter how hard I worked, I was never able to obtain success and keep it. Even when I achieved certain levels of success, I couldn't hang on because in my heart I believed a lie. I always found a way to get rid of it (self-sabotage). The feeling I did not deserve success kept me from moving forward. On the other side of the issue, are those who are so driven by success they become consumed by it. Their experience is opposite to mine. They achieve success at the expense of all else. Their pursuit of success is accomplished at the expense of family and friendships and real influence. They give up true love and acceptance for the illusion of wealth and success. They've made money into their God.

Both are dangerous. Both are symptoms. The fear of success and the idolatry of success both put themselves at the center of everything. Two very different methods of getting you into the same place. A life without God at the center. Both of these symptoms will leave you wanting and unfulfilled, constantly looking for approval, acceptance, security, and identity which can only be found through Christ. Neither of these things allow the love of your Heavenly Father to take you into a place where you can achieve your true purpose and fulfill the calling and destiny you know in your heart.

Your first step is to believe the promises God has spoken to you. The Scriptures show God loved you so much He formed you, created you, and designed you, before you became a being in your mother's womb. That is how much your Heavenly Father thinks about you. I suggest you ponder those words for a moment and grasp the reality of what He's put into you. Allow the Holy Spirit to minister this truth to you—how much He loves and cares for you. Feel free to put this book down while you ponder and pray over this very important aspect of your faith.

And I am convinced that nothing can ever separate us from God's love. Neither death nor life, neither angels nor demons, neither our fears for today nor our worries about tomorrow—

not even the powers of hell can separate us from God's love. No power in the sky above or in the earth below—indeed, nothing in all creation will ever be able to separate us from the love of God that is revealed in Christ Jesus our Lord.
Romans 8:38-39

What is the ultimate plan God had in mind before He put us on the earth? In an earlier chapter we saw a picture of the perfect spirit-filled life in Genesis chapter 2. God formed man and breathed into his nostrils the breath of life. The word "breath" literally translated, is "spirit." God placed His Spirit in man to give him life from the beginning. He then placed Adam in charge of the garden. Adam, the first man in our lineage was created to take dominion over the earth, which he did very well for a while. God knew from the beginning if His people properly controlled the finances of this earth, living in His prosperity and increase, they would be an unstoppable force who would cast out the darkness, set the captives free, and bear fruit increasingly for the kingdom.

From the very beginning, God planned for you to prosper. You can see continuous prosperity in our forefathers Abraham, Isaac, and Jacob, each one of them wealthy beyond reason. The Bible says between Abraham and Lot there was strife because they were so prosperous, the land could not contain them (Genesis 13:6). Even when Lot got into trouble and was hauled away captive, Abraham was so prosperous that his people were a greater force than the army of five kings who held Lot captive. Abraham set Lot free. (Genesis 14) Now that's prosperity. Isaac was also very prosperous. Genesis chapter 26 says Isaac, as a favored son of God, was able to plant a crop in a land consumed by famine, and he reaped a one-hundredfold crop. This is the kind of prosperity God plans for you.

Jacob began his life as a deceiver, and he served his uncle Laban for decades. But early in his life Jacob made a covenant with God. Genesis chapter 28 says Jacob made a covenant with God and promised to always give a tenth of his increase. Later, when Laban was doing everything he could to cheat Jacob, God prospered Jacob's flocks and herds more than Laban's. God the Father, wanted Jacob to prosper more than the world.

Joseph prospered even while in prison, and was eventually appointed as ruler over the land. He governed as the right hand of Pharaoh during a time of great abundance and then great famine in Egypt. During the famine things grew so dire the Egyptians sold their livestock and their land to Pharaoh. They gave everything they owned just to be able to eat. Even during this time, the entire nation of Israel prospered. The Bible records them as owners of land in Goshen. While the world was starving and selling all their possessions just to eat, God's people continued to prosper, being owners of land and receivers of wealth.

Even after 400 years of slavery, when God reached down to deliver His people from the bondage of slavery to Egypt, the first thing He did was cause the Egyptians to give them their gold. (Exodus 12:35-36) This is certainly proof that even in a time of transition, God plans for His people to prosper.

Deuteronomy chapter 11 speaks about the Promised Land, and how God promises the land will bring the rain which yields crops for abundance. God's promise always brings increase. The Bible is full of story after story showing how God's plan is to bless and prosper you. The more time you spend in His Word the sooner you will discover His plans and hear from God yourself.

If you listen to these commands of the Lord your God that I am giving you today, and if you carefully obey them, the Lord will make you the head and not the tail, and you will always be on top and never at the bottom. Deuteronomy 28:13

The promise in this verse even defies the condition of the financial markets. It clearly says you will be on top and never at the bottom. When you remain grounded and rooted in God's plans and promises you will continue to be blessed, and He will give you increase and provide for you no matter what is going on in the economy. This promise explains how Isaac was able to sow in a time of famine and reap a one-hundredfold crop. Because of this promise, Jacob was able to grow and prosper while Laban schemed to cheat him. And it is because of this promise, in a time of crisis in Egypt, the people of God were able to walk out of the city with the Egyptians' gold.

It is up to you to believe in the Father's good pleasure to give you the kingdom. His Word is His promise to you. The more you receive and accept this truth in your life, the more you will be able to prosper, regardless of the world's economy. But it all starts with your perception of yourself. Decide now to accept the truth of your identity, and the purpose God the Father has put in you. By accepting and walking in His promises, you will enjoy all the prosperity He desires to give you.

Chapter 8

The Power of Vision

Faith is a key element to financial success. I can't emphasize enough, no matter what you believe, you will receive. If you believe for lack, then you will receive lack. Therefore, it is important for you to start building your faith correctly.

I tell you the truth, if you had faith even as small as a mustard seed, you could say to this mountain, 'Move from here to there,' and it would move. Nothing would be impossible.
Matthew 17:20b

Today, it seems more prevalent to believe in lack. It certainly is easier. Perhaps that's why 96% of people today reason they cannot accomplish their goal because they don't have enough money. It is an excuse to stop trying, to justify a lack of action. The energy expended in making excuses would be better spent working to build faith for achieving a dream.

Remember there is still 4% of the population who know the truth and achieve financial success anyway. They've learned to believe **pro**vision comes after **the** vision. They believe if they can dream it, then they can achieve it. That is faith. While this small percentage of people achieve great things, the majority of people live a life which falls far short of their potential. The sad part is, not only do they miss the opportunity to fulfill their purpose, but in the process, they also program their kids for the same life of mediocrity.

When people do not accept divine guidance, they run wild.
Proverbs 29:18a

Another translation says, "Where there is no vision the people cast off restraint." People who live without a purpose are people who have no reason to plan and discipline themselves to build for the future. In this passage, you could substitute the word "vision" with the word "dream." Then it would read, "Where there is no dream, the people lack discipline." Specifically, the discipline needed to pursue a dream. You need to give yourself permission to dream again. Do you remember what it was like to dream when you were younger? It may take a moment, but if you stop and think, you could recall some of the dreams of your youth. What happened? Why did you stop dreaming? Why did you stop planning for your future? The answer could very well be, you grew up!

I remember times transitioning from a teenager to a young adult and my teachers would tell me to grow up and get serious about life. They told me to stop dreaming and start being responsible. You probably heard the same thing. What's even worse, you have probably said it to someone else.

Why did you give up your dreams and decide to accept this thing called responsibility? It's because you entered the real world. The adult world has bills to pay and requires an income. Unfortunately for some, your job can become a prison too difficult to escape. But it's only a prison if you let it be. Here is where you find the importance of vision. Vision is birthed from a passion God places in your heart. When your career is connected to the passion in your life, even your job will fulfill the purpose God created you for.

How do you step from prison to passion? The answer is simple. Give yourself permission to dream again! Allowing yourself to dream means trusting God to make provision for your dreams to come true. Those 4%ers who achieve financial success dream! They dream. They take action. They move toward their dream. They believe provision will always come to provide what they need for their vision. The 96%ers wait for provision to come before they begin pursuing a dream, which is completely backward. This approach lacks faith and goes against the commandments of God. In the opening verse, Jesus said faith comes first as a mustard seed before it ever becomes a tree.

The provision you're waiting for needs a vision to bring it into existence. The word, "provision," has a simple breakdown. The word "pro" means in favor of or in support of, while the word "vision" refers to a dream or a revelation. Therefore, provision is in support of a dream or revelation. From this understanding, you can see the vision or dream must come first. Then the means to make it a reality will follow. This is how God intended for our lives to work, and Jesus teaches this throughout Scripture.

And he called his twelve disciples together and began sending them out two by two, giving them authority to cast out evil spirits. He told them to take nothing for their journey except a walking stick—no food, no traveler's bag, no money.
Mark 6:7-8

Notice in this important passage Jesus himself gathers His disciples together and gives them a vision. He tells them He's sending them out, two by two, and gives them the power to set people free. Then, once He knows they understand the vision, He adds an extra challenge. He tells them they are to go and take nothing with them. No money, no food, no Bibles or tracts, or prayer cloths, or ministry tools of any kind. They are only to go themselves and trust God for what they need along the way.

Jesus clearly painted a picture of what he wanted his disciples to do. He also wanted them to exercise their faith. So He sent them with nothing, to show them God would provide for every need they had along the way.

And don't be concerned about what to eat and what to drink. Don't worry about such things. These things dominate the thoughts of unbelievers all over the world, but your Father already knows your needs. Seek the Kingdom of God above all else, and he will give you everything you need. Luke 12:29-31

Again, Jesus is telling you not to worry about provision because He has already taken care of it. He is encouraging you to pursue the dream He has placed in your heart and to trust Him to make provision along the way. This wisdom is contrary to what the world says. The world wants you to look before you leap, and although there is wisdom in evaluation, there is not much faith involved. The world says not only look before you leap but anticipate the cost of a safe landing. Here is the place again where your bank account dictates your action. It is the lie of mediocrity which keeps you from reaching your potential.

This is not a recommendation to be reckless, but an encouragement to take risks. You can jump with confidence when you pray over possible risks and know God's plan in advance. Jesus said in Luke 19:26, risk your life and get more than you ever dreamed of, play it safe and end up holding the bag. (MSG)

My people are being destroyed because they don't know me. Hosea 4:6a

The more you know the Word of God, the more you know Him. The more you know Him, the more you understand how God intends for you to live your life and the more successful you will be. A lack of understanding can cause you to forget your dreams while waiting for provision. A lack of understanding can cause you to believe our own excuses. Remember your excuses are nothing more than reasons to justify a lack of action.

As outlined in the last chapter, your identity as a child of God is key. God gave me a picture of identity one day. He showed me a prince who lived in the capital city with his father the king. Although the prince lived in the castle, it was not uncommon to see him walking in the streets of the city. The people who lived in the city saw the prince quite often, so whenever he spoke, the people recognized who he was and obeyed his command. The prince's authority as the son of the king came easily in the capital city where he lived.

One day the king asked the prince to go to a city in a far-off province to take care of some business for him. After several days' travel, the prince arrived in the strange town. Although he was far from home, the prince was still in a city under the authority of his father the king. The prince had never been seen in this city before, but he was still prince of the land with the same authority as in the capital city.

Unfortunately for the prince, the people of this town knew he existed, but they had never seen his face. Consequently, they did not recognize him when he arrived. This proved to be challenging for the prince. He walked around the city, knowing in his heart he was still a son of the king, but he could not understand why the people did not recognize his authority as they did back home. The prince began to question his identity, and along with it, his authority. Was he really meant to do a job in this town? How could he accomplish the task his father sent him to do? The answer was found in his identity as the son of the king. As a son of the king, he had the same authority even if the people did not recognize him. So what did he do? He sent a message to the king who dispatched a proclamation to the far-off city, declaring the authority of his son. When the prince showed the proclamation to the people, they obeyed his commands.

The sad part of this story is the prince had proof of his authority all along. If he had been bold enough to tell the people who he was, they would have noticed his royal robes and become subject to his commands. It was not because the people failed to recognize him that he was unable to complete his mission. It was because **he** failed to recognize his own identity and take the proper authority over the situation on his own. In many ways, you are like the prince. You carry the authority of your Father in Heaven, yet when His presence is not recognized, you cower and question your own identity. Without identity, you will not only fail to dream, but you are more easily led astray.

Go back and take a look at Adam and Eve in the Garden of Eden. You know how the story started. The two were created and placed in the garden to live a happy life in the presence of God, but then the serpent asked some questions. Since the dawn of time people have wondered, why did Eve eat the fruit? The answer has many layers, but I want to focus on identity. Eve was not confident in who she was! Let me show this to you.

Then the man—Adam—named his wife Eve, because she would be the mother of all who live. Genesis 3:20

Adam named his wife Eve after the deception. Imagine for a moment how different this might have been if Adam had done his job as her husband and provided her an identity by giving her a name before the devil started asking her questions. After all, it was Adam's job to give a name to every living creature, (Genesis 2:19) yet somehow, he didn't give his wife a name right away. I submit to you, if Adam had given his wife a name, solidifying her identity before the serpent came with his questions, it could have changed the scene. She might have better understood the authority she carried and not been led astray. She could have seen the serpent for the snake it was and crushed it for being a distraction from her true purpose. It is easier to stay focused on your vision and your calling when you know who you are.

Being solid in your identity is a key to unlocking your dreams and your vision. A clear vision allows you to see a prosperous future ahead.

Your eye is like a lamp that provides light for your body.
When your eye is healthy, your whole body is filled with light.
But when it is unhealthy, your body is filled with darkness.
Luke 11:34

It was a vision of the Father's promise which gave Jesus the strength to endure the cross. It was a vision of the glory ahead which gave Paul the strength to run his race. And it will be your vision giving you the faith to endure and overcome your current challenges. Joel 2 describes the saints of God.

Fire burns in front of them, and flames follow after them.
Ahead of them the land lies as beautiful as the Garden of Eden.
Behind them is nothing but desolation; not one thing escapes.
Joel 2:3

This is a picture of vision. Notice how the people described in this passage are looking toward the promise ahead. They see everything ahead as if it is the Garden of Eden. This is how to focus on a positive vision. Notice also everything behind them is seen as a desolate wasteland. They are not allowing anything from their past to hold them back. They have cast away all past mistakes and have accepted the redeeming love of God. They are focused on His promise ahead, and they are running toward it! This is the power of vision!

I want to focus on some people who allowed their dream to carry them beyond the obstacles of their time. These people had challenges from their past which could have easily held them back, but they chose to look ahead and focus on the promise. If anyone was given a dream by God, it was Abram.

The Lord had said to Abram, "Leave your native country, your relatives, and your father's family, and go to the land that I will show you. I will make you into a great nation. I will bless you and make you famous, and you will be a blessing to others. Genesis 12:1-2

How crazy was this vision? First, a man claims he heard from God. This happens to be a God nobody else in the land knew at the time. This is crazy but it keeps getting crazier. Not only did Abram hear from God, but he was told to leave his home **and** he would become a great nation of people. How about that for one crazy vision!

God blessed Abram in all he did and prospered him along the way. It took great faith for Abram to leave his homeland and chase this crazy dream. It was his faith which pleased God so much He came to Abram one day and made a covenant with him. As part of the covenant, God changed Abram's name to Abraham. (Genesis 17:15) Today we know our forefather Abraham as the man the Bible calls, "the father of all those who believe." (Romans 4:11)

There are many stories of great men and women who followed Abram's example and lived a life of faith in Hebrews 11. There are also examples of great men of faith and vision found in our history books. One of my favorite stories is about George Washington Carver. He was a man who faced steep obstacles in his life. He overcame them because his vision and his faith in God were larger than any of the obstacles he faced.

George Washington Carver was born a slave. When he was a young boy, his mother was sold away from him leaving George an orphan. Even though slavery was abolished early in his lifetime, racial discrimination created some very big obstacles for young Mr. Carver. In spite of these obstacles, George Washington Carver pursued his dream. It is recorded that he would get up early in the morning to pray. He spent time with God and as a result, he understood his identity. He was given the strength to pursue the purpose and vision God placed in his heart.

His dream came from a need he saw, and the desire to provide a solution to a problem. The boll weevil was a little bug which left destruction in its wake. Primarily cotton crops were damaged which adversely affected the economy of the south which depended heavily on cotton. George Washington Carver spent a lot of time researching and promoting alternative crops to cotton. He wanted to find ways for poor families to grow crops which would provide both food and income to help them prosper. His research promoted crops like soybeans and sweet potatoes, but he is most noted for his work with the peanut.

Mr. Carver developed 105 food recipes using peanuts. He also developed over 100 products made from peanuts. History records Mr. Carver asked God to show him ways for people to use the peanut. As I said earlier, God loves to show off. Among the contributions Mr. Carver made, his products included cosmetics, paint and dyes, plastics, and even gasoline and nitroglycerin.

As a result of George Washington Carver's diligence in pursuing his dream, he was accredited with many useful inventions and was widely honored for his work. He was asked to testify before Congress, he met with three US presidents, and was visited by the crown prince of Spain. In his day, Mr. Carver was considered an honored guest of many wealthy and well-connected families. When you consider the world he grew up in, you cannot deny the prosperity he walked in. He was a black man honored during a time of great discrimination and racial segregation, which was nothing short of a miracle! The power of pursuing your dream and putting your trust in God is limitless.

So what is your dream? What is buried down in your heart that you would start doing right now if money was no object? This is the question you need to start asking yourself right now. If money was no object, what would you do? Dreaming is easy when you take money out of the way.

Take some time to ask God for a renewal of your dreams. Trust He will be faithful to release even more dreams to you. Then, give yourself permission to dream again. Next, grab a journal and start to write down your dreams. No matter how big or how crazy it may seem. Write them down. Dreams are made a size too big so you can grow into them.

Then the Lord answered me and said: "Write the vision And make it plain on tablets, That he may run who reads it.
Habakkuk 2:2

Now is the time. Believe God to restore your dreams! Take the vision He gives you and write it down. Then pray over your vision and pursue it, knowing God will make a way for it to become a reality.

Chapter 9

Take Back Control

If you don't take control of your money,
your money will take control of you!

I know what it's like when finances are completely out of control. The feeling of no matter how hard you work you just can't get ahead. I've been there! But the good news is, it doesn't have to stay that way.

I've been through some tough times with my family. We've been through bankruptcy, and we lost the first home we bought as a family to foreclosure. Believe me when I tell you these were stressful times. The most difficult times were when my girls were little. The three of them were so close in age it seemed as soon as we entered a particular phase of their lives, it continued for years (one right after the other). Imagine having three little girls in diapers all at the same time. It was challenging to say the least.

As they grew, their needs changed and so did the demands on our finances. It seemed the older they got, the more expensive they were. A 2023 study done by smartasset says it costs an average of $20,813 per year to raise a child in today's society. If you multiply times 18 years, we find an average of $374,634 to raise a child from birth to age 18. Because I have three daughters, I needed to generate a little more than 1.1 million dollars just to raise them. This statistic only includes basic necessities, not all the other expenses of life, such as a home or a car. Let's not even get started on vacations or anything which sounds like fun. Adding those things makes the amount even greater.

If you have kids, you know just like I do there are certain expenses which cannot be avoided. One of my favorite examples is the afternoon my wife called me in absolute hysterics. I could barely understand what she was saying, but somehow in between sobs and screams, I managed to decipher that my oldest daughter had crashed on her skateboard. Naturally, I rushed home to see what all the panic was about and discovered when my daughter crashed her skateboard, she went face first into the sidewalk and broke off her two front teeth at the root.

As a father I felt the pain of my baby girl, but as a provider I began to wonder how I was going to pay for this. At the time, we had no savings account and no dental insurance to cover such emergencies. But I knew I couldn't let those things stop me. My baby girl needed attention and she needed it immediately. Today, I realize those are the kind of challenges life can throw at us every day. But at the time, all I was concerned about was the cost. And to cover the cost, I used my credit card.

I'm not completely against credit cards, quite the contrary. In today's society you need to have a good credit rating, which means you need to learn responsible use of your credit cards. Instead of using them to purchase fruitless things, I started using credit cards to cover life's little emergencies—like my daughter's broken teeth. This works well in theory but in reality, even the practical use of credit cards can get out of control. The plan of mammon outlined earlier is to put you into debt and bondage to your money. Even when you get your money under control, life's little mishaps can become mammon's leverage to open the doors and come back into your life.

It took me a few years of dealing with life's little catastrophes to again build up a sizable amount of debt. It was hard for me because I had already learned to hate debt. I learned to see it for exactly what it is—a direct attack from the enemy to put me into bondage and make me powerless. But even with my hate for debt, I still found myself deep in it.

This time the debt was different from before. I did not build it up by overspending on electronics, or vacations, or new cars. In fact, I didn't even have a car payment at this time since we owned our cars outright. In this case my debt was caused by life's little emergencies I had chosen to charge on my credit cards. And the very real danger for me was falling into the excuse trap. The excuse of my debt being a necessary part of life. There was a danger of being convinced again I would never have enough money to pay for unexpected things. The danger was falling prey to a dependence on my credit cards.

This philosophy is contrary to the Bible. The Bible promises God will supply all of your needs. This means if you are relying on a credit card, you are not trusting God. Taking this one step further, if you are not trusting God, then you are limiting His ability to provide for you. Here is the main, foundational issue. I was limiting God's ability to take care of me according to the promises of His Word.

Look at the birds. They don't plant or harvest or store food in barns, for your heavenly Father feeds them. And aren't you far more valuable to him than they are? Matthew 6:26

Although I had heard this scripture many times, I never quite understood it until the Lord opened up a revelation to me. The Scripture says to consider the sparrows, which is the easy part. Birds fly around in the sky as if they don't have a care in the world. Birds gather worms, build nests, and live what seems to be a pretty content life. And hearing birdsong just makes you feel happy. Notice what Jesus says next! This is such a powerful statement. He points out the sparrows don't plant or harvest or store food in barns. Here is the kicker. The sparrows do not have businesses. They do not plant crops in the field. They do not have a savings account to take care of them on a rainy day. They have no provision for life's little emergencies. Yet, they never lack what they need. Let this sink in for a moment!

Consider your ways. Most people are taught worldly wisdom. Wisdom which says you must go to school and get a good education. Next you must work in your career for a company that pays well so you build up savings and make some investments. Worldly wisdom is vastly different from the life of a sparrow. The sparrow simply pursues its passion and lives the life it was created to live. This is a lesson we can learn.

During a sparrow's life it must gather food and provide for its young, just like we do. This follows the biblical principle saying if you don't work you don't eat (2 Thessalonians 3:10). But the sparrow is not involved in the harvest. This is a kingdom economic principle you need to grab. You need only be sufficient for the day, then rely on God and trust Him to provide (Matthew 6:34). If your Heavenly Father provides for the sparrow, God will do the same for you, if you let him.

There is another example of this in the Old Testament when Israel came out of Egypt and crossed the wilderness toward the Promised Land. The wilderness was a desert. There wasn't any water to drink which is why God told Moses to draw water from a rock. (Exodus 17:6) There was also no food to eat, so God caused Manna to fall from heaven. (Exodus 16)

We clearly see in these two examples how God has already met your needs. When you put your faith in bank accounts and credit cards, you deny God the opportunity to be a provider. And this was the trap I fell into and why my debt had built up again. I was not trusting God to provide. I had turned to my credit cards and the world's system to meet my needs instead.

The problem was now my debt had taken control. It had put a strain on my finances once again and I felt I would never get ahead. I needed a change! Thankfully, my Heavenly Father has everything I need. All I needed to do was call on Him.

Is anyone thirsty? Come and drink— even if you have no money! Come, take your choice of wine or milk— it's all free!
Isaiah 55:1

Those words from God simply say you cannot put a price on His provision. He does not charge you for His provision, but He instructs you to come and buy the things He has for you without money. He says come and buy wine, which represents His teaching and His word. He says come and buy milk which represents the solid foundation that can only be built upon His word. And He says come and buy it without money and without price.

I came to realize if God was telling me to come to Him without money, He would give me all I needed. All I had to do was trust Him at His Word. When I did, I discovered His grace is sufficient for me (2 Corinthians 12:9). God's promise of provision and my acceptance of His grace was all I needed to change my current circumstances. This begs the question, if God is willing to give you such grace, then what exactly is grace? The definition of grace is the unmerited favor of God. If God's grace is unearned favor, then all you have to do is accept it. Whether you think you deserve it or not, it is still yours to accept.

For me, accepting God's grace also meant submitting to His guidance which meant I had to make some changes with my finances. So I started to cry out to God and ask for help. I began to realize if God's plan was to take care of me, even in the middle of the wilderness, then He must have a way for me to escape my financial turmoil. And my turmoil was completely out of control. I worked hard all week and got paid on Friday, but it seemed every paycheck was spent before I received it. I was essentially broke again by Saturday, and the cycle seemed never ending. I just knew it had to stop.

I decided to trust God and accept His grace. I sat quietly at my desk one day and began to pray. It was in this quiet moment God shared something else with me. He told me to make a list of my income and expenses and share the list with my wife, which was a new concept for me. Although we had been married several years, I had always taken care of the finances and never really shared them with her. Now God was telling me to go over our household budget with her. I wanted to make sure I was hearing God right. I continued to pray about it for a couple more days, but His message to me stayed the same.

Finally, I obeyed. I sat down at my desk, and I made a list of all of our expenses in one column, and I listed all our income on a single line in the other column. It was not a very pretty list, but I showed it to her anyway. I'll never forget that day. My wife and I sat down, and I told her what God had told me. I carefully went through each item with her, explaining what every expense was as we totaled them up together. Then I pointed to the single line on the income side which showed how we did not make enough to cover our expenses.

Before this conversation there was quite a bit of strife between me and my wife. She would buy a gallon of milk and a loaf of bread because the kids needed food. Then I would yell and scream because she had spent money that only I knew we didn't have. It was not a very happy time in our relationship. But all changed when I showed her my list. I will never forget the look on her face as she realized the severity of our financial circumstances. Her first comment to me was, "No wonder you're always biting my head off."

By showing her the list, I'd opened the door for God's grace to come into our house. It gave my wife an understanding of our financial situation, then we were able to lock arms together and stand to face the fight. This was just the beginning. We had a newfound peace in our home due to the openness with our finances. We had a new unity in our relationship as we came together to wage this war. And war is exactly what it was.

Perhaps because of this experience, I see finances as spiritual warfare. Probably the most powerful spiritual warfare you will ever fight. The enemy knows if he can control your finances, then he has control over you. This is why I am encouraging you to fight and win in the financial realm and reign as kings over your finances.

Or what king would go to war against another king without first sitting down with his counselors to discuss whether his army of 10,000 could defeat the 20,000 soldiers marching against him? Luke 14:31

For those of you about to go to battle over your finances, you also need to count your soldiers—your dollar bills—and make an accounting of where your soldiers have been allocated. If they've all been directed to the wrong fields of battle, there's no way to win the war.

This is what the Lord of Heaven's Armies says: Look at what's happening to you! Haggai 1:5

God is telling you to look at what's happening in the same way Jesus said to look at the birds. Both passages are telling you to take a look at your own heart. The next verse continues:

You have planted much but harvest little.
You eat but are not satisfied. You drink but are still thirsty.
You put on clothes but cannot keep warm.

Your wages disappear as though you were putting them in pockets filled with holes! Haggai 1:6

This passage sums up exactly how I felt when I set out to wage war on my finances. I felt as if I was working hard, sowing a lot of effort into my career yet was still not satisfied. Even though I earned a good salary, it felt as if it still went into bags with holes. No matter how fast it came in, it seemed to go out even faster. You may feel the same at times as well. That's why God says, pay attention to what's happening.

With money, the first step to considering your ways is to submit to God, just as I did when He told me to make a list and share it with my wife. My obedience brought His grace, and peace returned to my home. The second part of the battle began when my wife and I stood together looking at our finances. We knew we had holes in our bags, and it was time to plug them. Plugging them started with climbing a ladder of accountability and accepting responsibility for our actions.

As human beings, there is a psychological ladder of accountability. At the lowest level is the tendency to blame others for unpleasant circumstances. Moving up to the next level is making excuses. The steps beyond making excuses reveal a void of waiting and hoping with no real substance. Finally, if you are truly searching, you will begin to acknowledge your reality and face the problems you have created yourself. Once you acknowledge and take ownership of the consequences of your decisions, you can enter into a partnership with God which allows you to begin to find solutions and win the war.

With the newfound peace in our home, my wife and I were finally able to take a clear look at our expenses and identify the problems. Just as the king mentioned in Luke 14:31, we started counting our soldiers and looking where they had been deployed. We accepted responsibility for the fact we spent more than we actually made. With this perspective the solution was simple. We had to find ways to spend less. With this mentality we began to wage war and plug the leaks in our bucket.

We sat down together reviewing our list of bills and discussed each item, looking for ways to reduce it. At this point we had already cut all the commonsense things like cable TV, dining out, and other unnecessary luxuries. There were still holes in our bucket, so we kept looking. This was a big one for us. We found we went to the grocery store 4 to 5 times a week. My wife and I looked at each other and wondered why we needed to go to the grocery store so often. We did our big shopping on Saturday so why did we have receipts from the grocery store again on Monday, Tuesday, and Thursday?

Obviously, we forgot things on Saturday, like for instance an extra gallon of milk. This meant we ran out of milk on Tuesday, justifying the extra trip. Now here is the problem. The milk is at the back of the store past all the fresh baked cakes, cookies, and desserts. On the way to the checkout, we would pick up a few extra things like chips or ice cream and before we knew it, a $3 gallon of milk turned into $30 at the checkout counter. Soon it was clear to us the milk was not the problem. The extra trips turned into unnecessary expenditures. Solution: planning our grocery shopping more effectively. We counted the number of meals throughout the week and when we went to the store on Saturday, we bought only what we planned for. We then made a rule for our house. No additional trips to the grocery store at all during the week, no matter what we thought we needed. The decision was made that if we didn't have something, we would wait until our next regular grocery day to get it.

This one simple strategy saved my family more than $400 each month. I know it sounds like a lot of money to save from something so simple but that's how it worked. Each one of those extra trips to the store cost us on average, $25-$30, multiplied three to four times each week, and four weeks in every month. You do the math. The first $400 in savings brought relief in our home along with a whole new level of joy and trust in God. All it took was letting God come into my life and be Lord of my financial plan.

God's plan is for you to let Him be Lord over everything. You are to submit to His Kingship in everything and ask Him for direction and guidance on how to best use it. When I came to this awful place with my finances, His Grace became the power which delivered me. He is here to do the same for you, and all you need to do is call on Him and ask Him to be Lord over your finances.

You hoped for rich harvests, but they were poor.
And when you brought your harvest home, I blew it away.
Why? Because my house lies in ruins, says the Lord of
Heaven's Armies, while all of you are busy building
your own fine houses. Haggai 1:9

This verse sums up the struggle I was having with my finances. I was trying to build my own house, to provide for my own style of life, and to live up to my own ideal of success. Haggai says it is God who blows away your wealth when you fail to use it to serve His purpose. The answer to the problem is simple. Submit your finances to God and start using them to honor Him. By doing so, you will be allowing God to become Lord over your finances and open the windows of heaven to provide for you abundantly. Keep in mind, there is a process leading to your deliverance from the bondage of debt and giving you victory to live in the abundance God has promised.

The previous chapters outline a path to follow for this process. Breaking the mindset of poverty, exposing the influence of the spirit of mammon over your finances and now stepping into a place of accountability. This is the place where you can invite God to be Lord over your finances. You have come to the place where God can show you His desires for your finances.

Before you read on, I encourage you to stop, ponder, and pray. Make a list of your finances just like I did. In one column put all your income and in the other list all your expenses. Remember no matter what your list looks like, do not be discouraged. Instead, start building your faith by putting your list on the altar before God. Then take the time to pray over it. If you're married, share it with your spouse and the two of you pray together. Welcome God's grace to come into your finances just as you've welcomed Him to come into your hearts.

Finally, ask God to mend the leaks in your bucket. He will give you strategies to seal the holes in your bag, then act on the plan He gives you. Remember, His grace is sufficient for you.

This is my command—be strong and courageous! Do not be afraid or discouraged. For the Lord your God is with you wherever you go. Joshua 1:9

Chapter 10

Giving is the Key

Give, and you will receive. Your gift will return to you in full—pressed down, shaken together to make room for more, running over, and poured into your lap. The amount you give will determine the amount you get back. Luke 6:38

The more my wife and I fought, side by side, in the war over our finances, the stronger our relationship became. We faced this battle together, and the quest to reign over our finances bound us together tighter than ever before. It is heartbreaking how many couples are separated due to financial problems, when in reality those problems can serve as a tool for God to bring you closer together. I am grateful for His work in my marriage.

We experienced newfound freedom in our relationship as we sat down together every week looking over our expenses and planning exactly what we would pay. It definitely helped to have a few hundred extra dollars in our budget after God opened our eyes and gave us a plan to stop the leakage. But we still had debt, which continued to hold us down.

When Proverbs says, the borrower is a servant to the lender, we knew exactly what it felt like. Every month my wife and I would plan how much we could pay toward our bills, yet every month we were still bound by our credit cards. As mentioned earlier, I'm not completely against debt. I don't believe God is against debt, either. He knew we would borrow at times, which is why He put rules in place to regulate it. In fact, the Bible instructs us to be generous and lend to the poor.

Good comes to those who lend money generously and conduct their business fairly. Psalms 112:5

Debt does have its place, but it is frivolous debt which needs to be avoided. This kind of debt builds up when you buy luxury items like big-screen TVs and extravagant vacations on your credit cards. This is bad debt. Good debt generates income. An example of good debt could be a small business loan an entrepreneur uses to buy inventory to sell in his business for a profit. Debt used to generate income puts money back into the local economy. Another example of good debt could be a loan to buy a rental property. The loan may generate a debt payment of $1,500 per month, but if the property generates $1800 or more in rent, it is generating increased income. These are examples of profitable debt, or what is generally called good debt.

The debt I had was not built with luxury items, but from the catastrophes of life. However, it was still bad debt because it generated no income. Just the opposite, it drained my income and prevented me from investing to increase my income. This is the debt I had come to hate. I hated the bondage it put me in. I was bound to a contract to repay the debt while restricting my ability to bring any increase. Debt which fails to generate income is dead weight, like a millstone tied around your neck. As long as you have bad debt, you cannot invest your money toward increasing your income. If you have bad debt in your life, you know exactly what I'm talking about. You know the choking feeling of a rope wrapped firmly around your neck.

As my wife and I sat down together and looked at our debt, we started formulating our own plan to pay it off. I figured since we owned both of our cars, we could use them as collateral against a loan to help us pay off the bulk of our debt. Then with our new consolidated payment, we would be able to pay extra against the loan to ensure it was paid off faster. This was the plan we came up with and on paper it worked out great. The only problem with our plan was the bank would not give us a loan. Although they agreed our cars had value and made good collateral, they felt we simply owed too much, and would not approve of us borrowing any more. It was discouraging to be turned down for a debt consolidation loan. The only reason we were applying for a loan was to pay off debt, and the bank turned us down because we had too much of it. Somehow it seemed unfair. We knew we had too much debt, which is why we wanted to consolidate, but for the bank we were too much risk.

Looking back now, it wasn't the bank's fault we got turned down for the loan. Today, I clearly understand it was God's protection for us to be turned down for a loan. He knew the loan was our own plan and not a good one. When our plan failed, we were left with only one option—to put our faith in God. The last chapter showed how God makes provision for you. My wife and I had already begun to understand and practice this revelation. I shared with you how our submission to His plan for our finances brought peace back into our home and marriage, and opened a plan to plug the leaks in our financial bucket.

In spite of God's clear demonstration of His grace over our finances, we still made the mistake of thinking we had to bear the burden of the debt we had created. We still functioned with a performance mentality, feeling we were responsible for fixing the problem we had created. That is contrary to the grace God freely gives to us. Let's look again at the story of Elijah in 1 Kings 17:8-16. This story is not centered on Elijah but on a widow who was facing financial problems of her own.

But she said, I swear by the Lord your God that I don't have a single piece of bread in the house. And I have only a handful of flour left in the jar and a little cooking oil in the bottom of the jug. I was just gathering a few sticks to cook this last meal, and then my son and I will die. 1 Kings 17:12

Verse 12 describes the feeling of hopelessness we discuss earlier. That was a feeling I could identify with. Here I was, trapped in debt which consumed my financial resources. I felt hopeless, without any chance of escape, just like the widow. She was getting ready to make their last meal preparing to die. She had no hope of escaping her circumstances. She knew very well her resources had run dry, and she had no means of acquiring more. My debt made me feel exactly the same way. It was consuming all my resources and left me feeling I had no means of getting any more. Fortunately for me and the widow, God had a plan!

But Elijah said to her, "Don't be afraid! Go ahead and do just what you've said, but make a little bread for me first. Then use what's left to prepare a meal for yourself and your son. 1 Kings 17:13

Take a minute to understand exactly what Elijah was asking this woman to do. She told him there was no more flour or oil to make a cake with—it was her last portion. The request made it seem like Elijah missed it when he asked her to make one for him first. What a bold request. It took a measure of faith to obey such a command, and maybe some pure desperation. Just like the widow, my wife and I had the same feelings as we faced our debt.

God taught me long ago how crisis forces change, and our debt had definitely created a crisis. I had reached the end of my ability to solve the problem I had created, and it was time for me to make a change. The widow was clearly also in crisis and had reached the end of her own ability. Through Elijah, she was asked to make a change. She was asked to be generous and give before she prepared food for herself and her son. What a huge change it must have been! Completely without resources, she felt her life was over, and she was about to starve to death with her son. And who was the strange man asking her to give something she didn't have to give? Yet she obeyed this outrageous request.

For this is what the Lord, the God of Israel, says: There will always be flour and olive oil left in your containers until the time when the Lord sends rain and the crops grow again! 1 Kings 17:14

The outrageous request was met with an outrageous promise from God through the prophet Elijah. God promised if she gave to Him, He would not allow her resources to run dry. When I saw this promise, I began to question my own giving and to wonder if God asked the widow to give up all she had, could He be expecting the same from me?

So she did as Elijah said, and she and Elijah and her family continued to eat for many days. There was always enough flour and olive oil left in the containers, just as the Lord had promised through Elijah. 1 Kings 17:15-16

You may have heard this story before, but have you ever tested the theory behind it? Until God opened my eyes to this truth, I had never even considered how it could apply to my life. What I was finally able to understand from this story was the power of giving offerings. Although I had been tithing for many years, I wavered when it came to giving offerings (gifts above the tithe). That is what the widow was asked to give, an offering.

You must set aside a tithe of your crops—one-tenth of all the crops you harvest each year. Deuteronomy 14:22

Tithes are paid on your income (crops). But the widow had no income to tithe on. However, she could give an offering! This is when the lightbulb came on for me. I understood God was asking me to make an offering during this time of personal lack. It was a bold request, but one I decided to obey. With this new decision to give extra offerings, my wife and I sat down and began to plan how much we would give. We already felt we didn't have enough, so deciding to give extra was challenging. Yet somehow, we knew honoring God's request would open up provision for us, just like He did for the widow.

And it is impossible to please God without faith. Anyone who wants to come to him must believe that God exists and that he rewards those who sincerely seek him. Hebrews 11:6

This is where obedience and faith walk hand in hand. If you don't step out in faith, trusting Him at His word, you cannot please Him. Faith and obedience linked together, activate the promises of God.

This is a story of provision, and how God provides. But how does that relate to debt? Provision is food and shelter, but how does this help pay off bad debt? There is another story of a widow to help bring clarification in 2 Kings 4:1-7.

One day the widow of a member of the group of prophets came to Elisha and cried out, My husband who served you is dead, and you know how he feared the Lord. But now a creditor has come, threatening to take my two sons as slaves. 2 Kings 4:1

Clearly this woman was in debt. Her debt had become a crisis threatening to tear her family apart. It was much like the financial problems caused by many divorces today. Her problem was a debt problem.

"What can I do to help you?" Elisha asked. "Tell me, what do you have in the house?" "Nothing at all, except a flask of olive

oil," she replied. And Elisha said, "Borrow as many empty jars as you can from your friends and neighbors. Then go into your house with your sons and shut the door behind you. Pour olive oil from your flask into the jars, setting each one aside when it is filled." ***So she did as she was told****. Her sons kept bringing jars to her, and she filled one after another. Soon every container was full to the brim! "Bring me another jar," she said to one of her sons. "There aren't any more!" he told her. And then the olive oil stopped flowing. When she told the man of God what had happened, he said to her, "Now sell the olive oil and pay your debts, and you and your sons can live on what is left over." 2 Kings 4:2-7*

Did you catch the important part? She obeyed the command God had spoken to her through Elisha. Her act of faith opened the door for God to settle her debts. And He did more than settle her debts, He gave her an abundance of provision to continue to care for herself and her sons.

We've just seen two examples where God asked someone to give from something they did not have. In both examples these women gave, and in both examples, God brought provision. The provision did more than put a meal on the table for one day. In both cases, the provision lasted for some time. In the latter example, the provision not only settled the family debts, but took care of their future.

These are not just ancient Bible stories. This is how God, in His mercy, sets people free from their bondage! He is the same God, yesterday, today, and forever. He will do the same for you. As I began to understand this principle, I saw the words of Jesus issuing me the same challenge.

Give, and you will receive. Your gift will return to you in full—pressed down, shaken together to make room for more, running over, and poured into your lap. The amount you give will determine the amount you get back. Luke 6:38

Although I had heard this scripture before, this time the words leapt off the page at me. I knew God was speaking directly to my heart. Not only did He speak to me that day, but He also issued a direct challenge in the last sentence of this verse.

The amount you give will determine the amount you get back. Luke 6:38b

This was something new to think about. In this passage, Jesus is saying He can only give to us as much as we are willing to give to Him. If we only give Him a little, then He can only help us a little. But if we decide to give Him a lot, then we open the door for Him to bless us greatly.

With this new challenge, my wife and I stepped up to the plate. We faced the crisis of our debt, which told us we needed to make a change. The change forced us to try the only thing left which was to pray and ask God for help. He responded by revealing truth in the stories I just shared, and then issued the challenge to give. A challenge I was determined to accept. With this new understanding, my wife and I made the decision to double our giving. We stopped looking at what we thought we could afford to give and chose to give twice the amount we had been giving. Let me be clear. We did not suddenly get extra money which allowed us to give. The amount of income we had when I made this decision was the same amount we had before. This meant if we didn't have enough to pay our bills before we decided to give extra, then this extra giving would make it even harder to pay them now.

The logic here does not make sense in the natural. Conventional wisdom would say the exact opposite. If you followed conventional wisdom, you would ask God to give you extra so you could give it back to Him. However, the Kingdom's Economy works opposite to conventional wisdom. In God's Economy, you give first and He will give back to you, hence, the need for faith. Trusting God in spite of your current circumstances.

Before my wife and I decided to double our giving, our plan to get out of debt was going to take a little more than a year. Our plan also required the consolidation loan which the bank turned down. Without the loan, it would have taken us even longer to pay off the debt, no matter how aggressive we were. Fortunately for us, God loves to show off. As soon as we determined to double our giving, we opened the door for Him to move on our finances and He did it! We started giving extra, even though we didn't have it, and just as God promised in His word, He started measuring back to us. It was with His measure that all of our debt was paid off within 45 days! God did for us, in six short weeks, what we could not do alone over the course of several years. Here is the power of giving!

I know this sounds unbelievable, but it actually happened. As we started giving more, God opened the windows of heaven and unexplainable things began to happen. First, we received a letter from the IRS stating an error had been discovered in an old tax return. They sent us a refund check for a little more than $3,000. Talk about the unexplainable! The IRS sending money back is a massive miracle. Shortly after this we received a letter from our insurance company apologizing for an error in their accounting. They had overcharged us on our premiums for several years, and we received another unexpected refund check.

There were also added opportunities for work and extra projects which helped to increase our income. It meant we had to work a little extra and even put in a few extra hours throughout the week, but we were happy to do it. We knew the blessing of added income would help us get to our goal sooner. And it was apparent the extra projects came from God because we had not asked anyone. Those opportunities sought us out. When something like this happens, there is no denying God's hand in the matter. All this came on us so quickly we could not explain it away as coincidence. We knew God was honoring His promise, and we knew we had to do the same. With each unexpected bonus, we applied all of it to our debt. I believe this was the only way to honor our part while He was honoring His Word.

What God did for us, He will do for you. He does not care how you got into debt. He only asks you to trust Him. People often ask me what they can do to improve their financial situation. Every time someone tells me their story of financial lack, I ask them if they are tithing and giving. Every time without fail, the answer is, no not really.

Before we go on it is important to understand the difference between tithes and offerings. First, the tithe is the most basic amount God talks about. The word tithe literally means tenth, so a tithe is giving 10% of your earned income to honor God. In this way you are acknowledging He is your provider, and you trust Him with your money. The Word says the tithe **belongs** to the Lord. Keeping it for yourself is unwise.

You must set aside a tithe of your crops—one-tenth of all the crops you harvest each year. Deuteronomy 14:22

An offering is anything above the tithe which you give of your own free will. Although God can and will ask you to give extra offerings, you should also plan to give them out of a heart of generosity. God loves a cheerful giver.

If you help the poor, you are lending to the Lord — and he will repay you! Proverbs 19:17

God once explained giving to me this way. He related giving money to the passing of time. No doubt you've heard the phrase, time is money. God used this concept to illustrate the importance of giving to me. He asked me one morning, "If every month has 30 days, how many hours are in each month?" I did the math and figured, 30 days in a month, 24 hours in each day make a total of 720 hours every month. "So how many of those days every month do you spend building the relationship with your wife?" God asked. "We spend time together every day," I replied. "Imagine if you only spend 10% of your time every month with your wife." This means each month, I would only spend 72 hours with her (just a little over 2 hours each day). "Now how healthy would your relationship be?" As I pondered the question, I had to accept our relationship would not be very good.

This is how I understood the point He was making. If I held my time to the same law I held my money, then sowing only 10% of my time into my relationship with my wife would cause our relationship to suffer. This revelation led me to believe if I continued to sow **only** 10% of my money into the fields where God directed me, then my relationship with Him would also suffer.

Of course, God wanted to show me even more, so He asked another question. "How about if you sleep an average of eight hours every day which means you're awake for an average of 480 hours every month. If you only give 10% of the time you're awake, then you're only putting 48 hours every month (1.6 hours each day) into your relationship. How healthy will your relationship be?" For me the answer was clear. I understood if I only put 10% of my time into my marriage, then my marriage would not survive. With this understanding, there is no need to argue whether I give 10% of my gross time or 10% of my net. Either one would result in a relationship lacking real depth and would ultimately be doomed to fail.

In this example, God was relating time to money. He was showing me 10% of my gross time would not make a strong relationship. Then He showed me 10% of my net time every month would make my relationship even weaker. This opens a valid question. If we stop giving even 10%, whether off our gross or net income, how strong is your relationship and trust in God? Personally, I want my relationship with the Lord to be as strong as possible. I have determined to pay tithes on my gross income, then reach even further by giving consistent, generous offerings. Do you want your relationship with God to be stronger? Trust Him and make it your immediate priority to give. Even if you think you have nothing, make a plan to give. I promise if you do, God will open the doors of heaven and make abundant provision for all you need or owe.

Honor the Lord with your wealth and with the best part of everything you produce. Then he will fill your barns with grain, and your vats will overflow with good wine.
Proverbs 3:9-10

Let me leave you with one final thought. The Bible says the tithe is devoted to the Lord (Leviticus 27:28). The word *devoted* literally means it is set apart for destruction. What this means for you is, if you're not tithing, the stipulated amount will be taken anyway. God demonstrated this to me very clearly. It was during a time when I thought I could not afford to tithe. One week our washing machine broke, and I had to call an appliance repair person to fix it. It was a very unexpected expense. The bill was almost exactly the amount of the tithe I had just withheld. God was showing me, even if I didn't give it to Him, it was still devoted to Him, and therefore set apart for His destruction. This is not a matter of being unable to afford to tithe. This simply means you cannot afford NOT to tithe.

Bring all the tithes into the storehouse so there will be enough food in my Temple. If you do," says the Lord of Heaven's

Armies, "I will open the windows of heaven for you. I will pour out a blessing so great you won't have enough room to take it in! Try it! Put me to the test! Malachi 3:10

Chapter 11

10 - 10 - 70 - 10

God blesses those who are humble, for they will inherit the whole earth. Matthew 5:5

Humility or meekness is defined as using less than your full capacity. Jesus demonstrated meekness in all areas of His life.

For he is sent by God. He speaks God's words, for God gives him the Spirit without limit. John 3:34

Jesus had the fullness of the Spirit of God, and through His many miracles, He demonstrated the unrelenting Power of God. Yet when He was faced with the cross, He chose to suffer through it in His humanity instead of using His power to escape His suffering. He was humility on display!

In finances you are called to be humble as well, meaning if you have a dollar, you should spend less than a dollar. It is contrary to today's consumer-driven society, but it is scriptural. If you are meek with your money, then you will spend less than you take in. If you spend less, then you will have more funds available to use when those bargain opportunities arise. Opportunities like a dream deal on an item you have wanted to purchase for your home. Maybe in the past you couldn't jump on a great deal because you didn't have any extra money. Herein lies the value of being humble with your finances. If you practice humility with your finances, when an opportunity comes, you will have the few extra dollars needed to take advantage of it.

An employee of mine called one day asking for a little extra work in return for a little extra pay. I asked him why he suddenly needed extra money. He told me he had found a great deal on his dream computer, but he didn't have the money to buy it. I also saw an opportunity here. I knew he really wanted the computer, and the only way he saw to get it was earning extra money. I had a couple projects which needed to be done. I made a deal with him to get some work done for a cut rate and I helped him get his dream computer. In this instance, my meekness with finances put me in a position to get a great rate on the completion of my project. At the same time, I helped my employee to get the computer he wanted. When it comes to finances, meekness/humility is probably the most ignored principle. It is a lack of humility which often lands you in debt. A lack of humility can also cause you to miss God-given opportunities for increase.

Demonstrating this to a group of young people, I issued a challenge. After sharing this principle of meekness with finances, I asked the group of young men to each take a $20 bill and put it in their wallet. I challenged them to hold on to the $20 and ask God to present them with an opportunity to increase it. The challenge was to keep it in their wallet until the opportunity presented itself. A few days went by, and I asked the group how many of them still had their $20 bill. Most of them never put it in their wallet, but the few who did still had it. As the weeks went by, I would occasionally ask each young man if they still had the $20 in their wallet. One by one they began to tell me they spent it on something else. A couple of them told me a need came up which required them to spend it. But in those cases, the need was something they should have planned for as a regular expense.

There was one young man who continued to hold onto his $20 and wait for God to present an opportunity. As promised, God came through. This young man had the opportunity to purchase a video game console. He'd run across someone who needed some extra money and was willing to sell the video game console at a greatly discounted price. The price was, believe it or not, $20. The young man was then able to sell the video game console to somebody else for around $50. He more than doubled his money. He did not miss the opportunity because he still had the $20 in his wallet. He practiced meekness and patience with his $20 and he was blessed with an increase in his finances.

Humility in finance always starts with a plan. Some call the plan a budget. Personally, I can't stand the idea of a budget. I find it restrictive and too easy to break. A budget feels like nothing more than a set of rules telling you what you can and cannot do. To me a budget is a law or form of control which brings death. That is no way to live at all.

The letter of the law kills, but the Spirit pours out life. 2 Corinthians 3:6b

My main dislike about a budget is the potential to slow down your progress. As mentioned earlier, *you* need to control your money instead of letting your money control you. If you submit to a budget which guides your every financial move, it just turns out to be a different kind of control. It's a little like trying to spend less time on social media. First you decide to cut back on FaceBook, only to find you are spending more time on Instagram. All you did was replace one habit with another, thus allowing the same controls to keep you trapped.

My recommendation, instead of a traditional budget taking control of your life, choose to practice meekness. Humility with your finances reflects a condition of your heart which brings life and creates opportunities which allow abundance to flow. I can't say it enough. The idea is for *you* to take control of your finances. You need to have a motivating factor deeply rooted within yourself. The motivating factor is the dream God places in your heart. Through this dream (your vision) you can start telling your money what it's supposed to do, not the other way around.

If you've made the commitment to give first, (see previous chapter), then you've already started the process of telling your money what it's supposed to do. The commitment to give first shows no matter what the circumstances, the first thing you will do is honor (give to) God. When you take control, you can look at the money in your hands and tell a percentage of it to go serve the will of God. In the same attitude of command, you can start telling the rest of your money exactly what it's supposed to do. This puts you in control. You are taking dominion over the resources God entrusted to you and removing the power of bondage your resources once had over you.

With this new revelation as commander of the resources given by God, I challenge you to start commanding your money. Like any good commander, you need a good battle plan. I call this plan 10-10-70-10. With this plan you break your spending into four categories similar to the list below. Your forces are made up of dollar bills. Your job as commander is to direct your dollar bills to the proper fields of battle. This is spiritual warfare at its finest. These percentages are for the amount left after you have paid your 10% tithe.

- 10% - Charity

- 10% - Pay yourself

- 70% - Household expenses

- 10% - Sharpen your ax

First of all 10% = Charity

On the front lines of this battle you send out your finest troops. Get this part right and you have practically won the war. On the other hand, if you mess this up you really have no hope at all.

Take a look at what happened after the battle of Jericho. In Joshua 6, the people of Israel are going to battle against Jericho, the first city in the promised land. I recommend you read the story of the miraculous victory God gave to Israel as they followed His commands and obeyed His plans of attack. God was also very clear in his instructions to Israel on what they were to do with all the spoils they collected after they won the battle.

Do not take any of the things set apart for destruction, or you yourselves will be completely destroyed, and you will bring trouble on the camp of Israel. Everything made from silver, gold, bronze, or iron is sacred to the Lord and must be brought into his treasury. Joshua 6:18-19

It was God's intention for the people of Israel to honor Him by giving everything from this first city back to God. (The first of 10 cities, so the first 10% belonged to God). But there was a guy who had a different plan. His name was Achan, and he kept some of the treasure for himself and hid it. With this selfish act he not only failed to honor and worship God by giving the first as God commanded, but he also brought trouble on the whole camp of Israel. Because of Achan's failure to honor God, the people of Israel lost what should have been a simple battle when they attacked the next city of Ai. (Read Joshua 7). Achan's disobedience made even a small battle impossible to win.

The people of Israel discovered Achan's sin and made it right. Once the treasure had been sent to God's treasury as commanded, Israel started winning battles again, and they went on to conquer more land. How many battles in your financial war have you lost because you failed to honor God and give to Him first? Your first command should always be to give. You command your first platoon to go to charity in service to God. With this first command, you open the doors for God to pour out his increase on your finances.

Honor the Lord with your possessions, And with the firstfruits of all your increase; So your barns will be filled with plenty, And your vats will overflow with new wine.
Proverbs 3:9-10 NKJV

Secondly 10% = Pay Yourself

The next command is to send some forces into reserve. You must learn to pay yourself! In the Old Testament, there was an agro-economic society. People made their living by farming. A successful farmer plants a crop in the spring and harvests it in the fall. He then takes a portion of the grain he harvests and stores it as seed to replant for a new crop next year. If the farmer does not store seed for next year, but instead grinds it to make bread for today, then he won't be able to plant a new crop. He and his family will not starve today, but they very well could next year. Farmers clearly understand the basic principle—you do not eat your seed.

The principle is not much different in the economy today. Your seed is money, and the harvest you bring in is your paycheck. Just like the farmer holds back seed to replant next year, you need to hold back a certain amount of your paycheck. You need to be able to plant, or invest, to gain an increase for your future. If you're not paying yourself, then you're guilty of eating the seed and you're robbing your family of a future harvest.

Paying yourself first also serves other purposes. It gives you a cushion to help take care of unexpected emergencies. A good example of an emergency is a flat tire which should never be a life-altering catastrophe. I cringe every time I hear a Christian blame the enemy for a flat tire. I'm not saying the enemy won't throw a few obstacles at you, but I hate to give him credit for flat tires he had nothing to do with. The truth is, tires wear out, and when they wear out, they go flat. Regardless of why the tire went flat, you should not be caught off guard by the unexpected expense. We all have those unexpected expenses come up. Remember my daughter who crashed her skateboard and broke her two front teeth? That was definitely an unexpected expense. When you pay yourself, you build up a savings account to give yourself a cushion. It empowers you to deal quickly with unexpected things without having to run for the protection of a credit card.

Paying yourself is undoubtedly a hard thing to do. Society has been thoroughly conditioned to spend money. Almost from birth you are greeted with the message to buy more stuff. There is a message which deceptively says, the more stuff you have, the happier you will be. This message brings about buyer's remorse. I know the pain of buyer's remorse. On more than one occasion I have eaten the seed from my own silo when I brought home something I didn't need after being convinced by a brilliant marketing campaign, I had to have it. In the end I found I didn't need the thing at all and regretted spending the money. No doubt you've felt this way too.

The day I reached a place in my life where I was tired of being without seed to plant, became the day I adopted a plan to pay myself first. The first step was to open a savings account, but I ran into a problem right away. My savings account was attached to my checking account. It would automatically pull money from my savings to cover any overdrafts. Consequently, every week I put money into savings, and every week I took it right back out. It was a vicious cycle which needed to be broken.

Here was our solution. My wife and I opened a savings account at another bank, which was not linked to our checking account, and we declined to have debit cards connected to it. By doing this we put ourselves in a position to guarantee our savings. Every week we put money into our savings account at this new bank. And because we did not have debit cards connected to it, we had to be physically present to pull any money out. Of course, If we needed money, it was available to us, but the extra effort required ensured we did not use it frivolously. This system of savings worked great for us. In no time our savings account grew from hundreds to thousands of dollars. In fact, it seemed to grow so quickly, it boggled my mind. I was amazed at how fast money seemed to multiply in this new, safe and secure savings account we had opened at the bank across the street. By not having immediate access to the savings, we imposed a level of discipline which forced us to be more intentional with our spending. The result was a silo full of seed we could plant.

If you are faithful in little things, you will be faithful in large ones. But if you are dishonest in little things, you won't be honest with greater responsibilities. And if you are untrustworthy about worldly wealth, who will trust you with the true riches of heaven? Luke 16:10-11

In Luke 19, Jesus tells the parable of a master who gives a sum of money to ten of his servants. Those servants were commanded to do business and increase the master's money. The sum, a mina, was equal to about three months of regular wages at the time. In this parable, the faithful servants multiplied their mina and were given more authority as a reward. But the unfaithful servant faced judgement. Of course, the key to the opportunity that was given to them all was the initial investment of that Mina.

Most opportunities require an investment, which is why you need a savings account. As our savings grew, God began to present opportunities. The first business we opened required an investment equal almost exactly to 3 months of my wages. The business started with three employees and grew to employ fourteen more. Three months of wages, allowed to build up in our savings account, became a seed providing income for many others. This business generated nearly three-quarters of a million dollars in its first year. It all started by paying myself first. Imagine what you could do if you had a savings account with three months' worth of wages. That amount could help launch the dream God has placed in your heart.

God's plan for increase requires stewardship. Stewardship is taking control of the resources God has entrusted to you. Controlling those resources by taking command and telling them exactly where to go and what to do. The more efficient you become at commanding your dollar bills, the more opportunities you will have to multiply them. Pay yourself first.

There is desirable treasure, And oil in the dwelling of the wise, But a foolish man squanders it. Proverbs 21:20 NKJV

Next step 70% = Maximum Household Expenses

Now you've begun to establish priorities for your finances, it's time to take a look at your expenses. I'm talking about your necessary household expenses. Those things you need to operate your home, like housing, groceries, utilities, fuel and other expenses necessary to support you and your family. By now you have probably made a list of your expenses. Your list may include credit card debt and other unnecessary expenses, but those will soon be eliminated. For now, focus on just your basic household expenses listed above with the addition of insurance, clothing and medical. Your normal, basic day-to-day bills.

Remember I don't care much for a budget. I'm not concerned with making a list of everything you think needs to be in the category of household living expenses. What I am more concerned with here is the percentage of your income allocated to cover these expenses and I recommend the percentage not be greater than 70% of your gross monthly income. Keep in mind, your goal is to take control of your money and tell it what to do. Don't get discouraged if your household expenses are already greater than 70% of your income. In fact, most people introduced to this plan are spending far more than 70% of their income on these expenses.

I want to pause for a moment and re-emphasize the importance of meekness in your finances. You may not be aware of Parkinson's Law, but it has a very dramatic effect. Parkinson's Law says that bureaucracy expands to fill its allotted time. Parkinson's Law applied to finances says, as your income grows the cost of your lifestyle will also grow. The more money you make, the more your lifestyle and related expenses will also increase. This law is clearly demonstrated on the bumper sticker reading, "He who dies with the most toys wins." This is diametrically opposite to 'using less than your full capacity'.

If you find your household expenses are more than the recommended 70%, that's OK for now. The important thing is to identify your current situation and start praying about how to change it. You may need to make some sacrifices for a season until you get things under control, but the small sacrifice you make today will mean years of peace and security for you and your family.

Several years ago, at a time when our business, and therefore our income, was flourishing, my wife and I dreamt of a newer and bigger home. We wanted to get out of our subdivision and move into a home on a lake offering more privacy. Since we were making really good money at the time, we felt we could afford anything, so we looked at a home with a price tag of well over $2 million. In some markets this was an average home, but where we lived at the time in Orlando, Florida, it was an extravagant price to pay for a home. It didn't take long to pick out the house, and although it needed some updating, it had everything else we wanted. It sat in the middle of 3 ½ acres, the backyard opened up to a private lake, and it had a mother-in-law apartment over the garage which would be great when family or friends came to visit. But something in our hearts was unsettled. We had a little check in our spirit warning us against buying this house and thankfully we listened.

Two years later the real estate market collapsed, and with it our business and income fell. We could easily have lost the house to foreclosure and faced the threat of homelessness for my family. I'm thankful we had the wisdom to listen to God and keep our household expenses under control. In doing so, we broke Parkinson's Law and chose to maintain a modest lifestyle instead. As a direct result of our decision, we had a comfortable home throughout the recession which began in 2008. And although there were some tough times, as I've already shared with you, we were able to recover and get back on track to build up savings and to reinvest in other opportunities God brought our way. Unfortunately, everyone had not listened to the warnings. We watched some dear friends lose their home and be forced to move their family into a hotel room. It was an unfortunate situation, but one which could've been avoided if they had been humble with their finances.

But don't begin until you count the cost. For who would begin construction of a building without first calculating the cost to see if there is enough money to finish it? Luke 14:28

Finally 10% = Sharpen your ax

The strategy of this plan will help you to allocate your resources and break your dollars into troops who will fight the battle more effectively.

Just to recap, take the first 10% and give it to God. This first step is difficult to begin and requires a good amount of faith. Putting your trust in God goes completely against the prevailing thought in society. It is without a doubt the most important part of the battle, but it will cause you to win the war. By making the commitment to give God the first of your income, you are opening the door for Him to give back to you. God gives seed to the sower (2 Cor 9:10), sometimes purely out of His mercy. But most of the time it is given to those who give to Him first.

The next troops are the 10% you now pay yourself. This is the seed you must store up until God reveals a field He wants you to plant. Without seed in your silo, you will never be able to plant a crop to reap a hundred-fold return.

Then the largest force to wage the war is your household expenses. Don't worry if your expenses are greater than 70% to start with, God will show you a way to get them down. Just ask Him.

Now the last 10% is the most fun allocation of troops because you get to spend this final 10% on yourself. That's right, this last 10% is for you. The ax in the following passage is *you*. You must invest in yourself.

Using a dull ax requires great strength, so sharpen the blade.
That's the value of wisdom; it helps you succeed.
Ecclesiastes 10:10

Here is the plan for your final 10%. Spend about half of it to treat yourself to something nice. Maybe it's a simple night out for dinner and a movie, or a more elaborate weekend away with your spouse. It doesn't matter what it is, just make sure it's an enjoyable activity which gives you a release from all the normal pressures of life. This is important because if you don't treat yourself nicely, it won't be long before you don't like yourself. You will become miserable, your attitude will kill your motivation and rob you of your dreams, which is simply not acceptable. You are valuable. Be kind to yourself and treat yourself to something nice once in a while.

No one hates his own body but feeds and cares for it, just as Christ cares for the church. Ephesians 5:29

With the remaining portion of your final 10%, you need to invest it in yourself. Do something to improve yourself. Invest in your education. Read a book to increase your knowledge. Take a class to improve your skill. Attend a seminar to increase your wisdom and make you more valuable on the job. The more you invest in yourself, the more skills and knowledge you acquire, the more valuable you are to the world around you, and the more opportunities God has to promote you.

10 – 10 – 70 – 10 is a simple formula to help strategically direct your soldiers and send them out to war. The rest is up to you! But the key is to partner with God in this plan. You will succeed in reigning over your finances if you submit to God and let Him reign over you. That is the proper chain of command in this war.

To acquire wisdom is to love yourself; people who cherish understanding will prosper. Proverbs 19:8

Chapter 12

Prepare Your Fields

Do your planning and prepare your fields before building your house. Proverbs 24:27

I've been teaching financial seminars since 2005, and the one common goal of those who attend is to make more money. I am amazed at the number of people who are already millionaires, yet still want to know how to make more money. Equally amazing is the number of people so deep in debt, that being dead broke would be a financial increase. They too, want to know how to make money, but the difference between these two groups is their mindset. One of them only knows how to work for money, while the other group is looking for additional ways to make money work for them. This is the most powerful truth I can share about money. You will either give your time and your life working for money, or you will make your money work for you. There is no middle ground. When you learn to make money work for you, each day you line up all your soldiers—dollar bills—and tell them to go make friends. When they are directed properly, they bring their friends home at the end of the day. That is my simplified picture of making your money work for you.

The concept is quite basic. It's even easier when you've taken control of your money and have command of your forces as delineated in a previous chapter. Taking control is the first step. The next step is learning strategies which will cause your money to increase. The secret to stepping into increase will look entirely different from the world around you. It is normal in society to seek a good income, buy a nice car and house, then make payments for life. Although this is not a bad plan, it ignores a key principle from the scriptures. Proverbs 24:27 indicates how planning and preparation are the beginning. First, invest in income growing strategies, then use the increase from those strategies to build your house. When you build in this order—planting and developing the fields before the house—then the house is often nicer than it would have been the other way around.

Before considering strategies, you need to understand that increase is a Kingdom principle. In the Kingdom, increase is expected. Increase is the principle referenced in Genesis 2 when God describes the perfect Spirit filled life. In previous chapters, you will recall the first of the four rivers in the Garden of Eden was called Pishon, which means increase. The fact that increase is mentioned first in God's original dwelling place shows the importance of increase in our spirit led life.

The Bible is full of great examples of increase. In Genesis 12, Abram sets out to pursue the vision God placed in his heart. In Genesis 12:10, Abram made his journey in a time of famine. Then, in the opening passages of chapter 13, Abram became very wealthy in livestock, silver, and gold. Here is a perfect example of the increase God intends us to walk in, regardless of the condition of the world economy. The same increase God intended from the beginning is still available today.

So there is a special rest still waiting for the people of God.
Hebrews 4:9

The *rest* spoken of here is the rest God intended His people to have as they entered the Promised Land. Because this rest is still available today, the increase God promised is also available today. It is therefore our responsibility to enter His rest and live in the increase God intended. Your goal as a steward of Jesus is to bring increase into His kingdom. In fact, it is more than your goal. It is your duty as a servant of the Most High God.

Be a Multiplier

I've never met a person who didn't want more money, but I have met a lot of people who wanted more money for the wrong reasons. Granted, there are a good number of people who want more money for righteous reasons. Most people who want money for the wrong reasons are afraid of risk. Most of those people have little to no seed to start with. However, those with righteous intentions tend to be more comfortable with risk, and coincidentally, they usually have a good amount of seed money to start investing with.

An investor is described as someone who commits capital in order to gain financial returns. This is exactly what Jesus commanded us to do in both the parable of the talents in Matthew and the parable of the minas in Luke.

The servant who received the five bags of silver began to invest the money and earned five more. Matthew 25:16

The first servant reported, 'Master, I invested your money and made ten times the original amount! Luke 19:16

In both parables, Jesus commends those who gained profit through trading, and gave them authority over cities. As believers and servants of Christ, we have a duty to take authority over our communities, cities and regions, and this parable shows how authority and influence come from financial increase. To further illustrate the importance of increase, notice the consequences of returning without increase.

Now throw this useless servant into outer darkness, where there will be weeping and gnashing of teeth. Matthew 25:30

If given a choice, I'm certain you would much rather be the servant who was blessed with abundance, than the servant who was cast into outer darkness with nothing. To become the servant blessed with abundance, it is important to learn to understand the market cycles and become better able to manage risk.

There is a principle in investing of buying low and selling high, yet somehow, people have become experts at buying high and selling low. Unfortunately, this is often the result of people failing to understand the market. J. Paul Getty, one of the wealthiest men of his generation, said he got rich from buying when everyone else was complaining and selling when everyone else was celebrating, which is the complete opposite of what most people do. Most people decide to invest in something after it has already gone up in value. Their decision to invest is purely emotional, based on the excitement from someone else's gains. What they fail to realize is the market cycle for that particular investment has already run its course. But typically, being driven by greed, they invest anyway and end up losing their investment.

Before you invest in anything, you need to understand that every market has its cycles. There are four cycles to the market and understanding them properly will help you profit more easily. Anyone who invests without this basic understanding will be making a purely emotional investment and will almost always lose money. This brings up a very important rule of business and investing—do not let your emotions get involved. You can be emotional about your family, but never get emotional about money. Always keep in mind, money is nothing more than a tool which requires proper use at the proper time, as the market will allow. Having a basic understanding of market cycles will equip you to know the time to sow seeds which will bring in an increasing crop, and the time to sell and harvest your profits.

Understanding Market Cycles

From the tribe of Issachar, there were 200 leaders of the tribe with their relatives. All these men understood the signs of the times and knew the best course for Israel to take.
1 Chronicles 12:32

When Issachar was born, his mother Leah gave him the name which means wages. She said in Genesis 30:18, *God has given me my wages.* Moses spoke a blessing over the tribe of Issachar in Deuteronomy 33:19 saying they would benefit from the hidden treasures in the sand. When Israel settled in the promised land, Issachar occupied a fertile plain and became farmers. As a tribe of farmers, they knew how to read the seasons and the times. It was this ability which brought increase for their tribe and for the nation of Israel. They knew when it was time to change and which direction to go because they had learned to read the signs and recognize the cycle they were in. And just as Issachar learned to read the cycles, you must also learn to read the cycles of today's market.

The first cycle of the market is the bottom cycle. This is where the value of a product, commodity, or investment, is at its lowest. It's no coincidence that interest in a product as an investment is also at its lowest in the bottom cycle. At the bottom cycle, there tends to be pressure in the market to keep the price from going up. Of course, this does not mean there is no demand for the product, it just means the demand at this time is not greater than the supply. The abundance of supply over demand puts the buyer in control of the price, which helps keep the market low.

The best values can be purchased at the bottom of the market, when prices are at their lowest. If you plan to buy low and sell high, you need to identify market bottoms, which create opportunities for good values and guarantee good returns on your investments. At the bottom cycle, almost everyone will tell you it is a risky investment and not to do it. This means you must be willing to do what others are not—start investing in the bottom cycle. Just like J. Paul Getty built a large fortune when he bought in the bottom cycles of the market, you can build wealth with this strategy. However, before you buy anything in any market cycle, you need to research the investment and pray to be sure it is an opportunity God has for you.

The next cycle the market enters is the up cycle. This is the cycle where both interest and demand for a particular product or market starts to increase. The increase in demand results in an increase in pricing, which drives up the value of the market. Many investors look for the beginning of an up cycle before they enter the market. By seeing an increased interest in the product, the investor knows an increase in values will typically follow. So, with a little bit of market research, a calculated entry into a market which has just begun its up cycle can also bring great returns on your investment.

Following the up cycle, the market will hit its peak. The peak cycle is the third of four market cycles, and the one which usually gets the most attention. It's at the peak of the market when everyone is most excited. This is the time when wise investors will sell, pulling out their profits and proudly share their story of victory. They want everyone to know they just won a battle in the war to increase their finances. It's at the peak cycle of the market when the news media also starts talking about financial gains, which catches the interest of the general population. Increased interest often causes a final uptick in price as the majority of unwise people, trying to be investors, begin to enter the market looking for quick returns.

At this time everyone is celebrating, and it is the time when smart investors sell. As J. Paul Getty has said, when everyone is talking about an investment, it is actually time to sell it.

In 2006, most of America was dreaming of getting rich in real estate. In fact, I heard so much talk about the real estate market that it seemed everyone was buying real estate. As a result of this excitement, the prices for housing across America skyrocketed.

I had been investing heavily in real estate. I had been both flipping and renting houses for several years. Then in the spring of 2006, I went with my daughter on a fourth-grade field trip. The trip required a two-hour bus ride to reach our destination. While on the bus, I had a conversation with the teacher who told me she and her husband were taking a $100,000 equity line against their home to invest in more real estate. One of her students jumped in and shared with excitement how his mommy and daddy were doing the same thing. I didn't know as much then as I do now, but I did know enough to realize, if the topic of conversation on a school bus during a fourth-grade field trip was about a particular investment strategy, then it was time to adjust my strategy. The real estate market had reached its peak and was getting ready to enter its final cycle. The next cycle for this market started about a year later.

The fourth and final market cycle is the downturn. This cycle always follows the peak and can come very abruptly, just as it did in the US housing market in late 2007. It is during the downturn cycle when prices decrease, sometimes very rapidly. This cycle is when people are desperately trying to sell and stop their losses from getting worse. It is also during this cycle when many savvy investors begin to watch the market to identify when it hits bottom. At the bottom is where the opportunity to invest at lower prices comes back around and begins the cycle all over.

For everything there is a season, a time for every activity under heaven. A time to search and a time to quit searching. A time to keep and a time to throw away. Ecclesiastes 3:1,6

A good steward who manages the resources entrusted to him by His Master, will recognize the cycle of the market and know when it is a time to keep, a time to throw away, or a time to gain on the investments he makes. The most important aspect of timing market cycles is the need to have God involved. It is His money after all, so ask Him how you should invest it. When you do, you will always be more successful. Keep in mind, to be a good investor you will need wisdom which can only come from God. His wisdom will lead you as you learn to recognize and follow the market cycles. Fortunately, it's not hard to identify what cycle the market is in. When you take a few minutes to look at the news, you can quickly see which direction the market is going. Of course, there is more involved in determining a good investment. This is where research and prayer are invaluable. Here are some basic investment options available to you.

Sowing Your Seed

There are three basic strategies anyone can use to build wealth. These strategies can be used separately, or in combination. Each of these vehicles operates by the same basic principle of faith. Faith says if you sow a seed into a field, it will grow a crop. But with faith you must also mix in knowledge and wisdom.

A house is built by wisdom and becomes strong through good sense. Through knowledge its rooms are filled with all sorts of precious riches and valuables. Proverbs 24:3-4

The first strategy is business. A business is defined as the practice of making one's living by engaging in commerce. To engage in commerce involves some risk, therefore you must exercise a measure of faith. Would you say it takes faith to buy a widget for $1 then take it to market to sell it for $3? After all, if you can buy the widget for $1, why can't everyone else? Here is where faith comes in. Faith is a substance which comes from a relationship with your creator. Faith starts first as a seed and then grows into a large, strong tree. The idea for a business is also a seed. When the seed is planted, it can grow into a large tree or even an orchard continuing to produce fruit. You may already have an idea for a great business. To get started you will also need a great plan. The plan is actually more important than the idea, because without a plan, even the best idea can fail.

If you have a desire to launch a business, you need wisdom, knowledge and a plan. If you don't have a solid plan but you still have a desire to own a business, you might consider buying a franchise. A franchise is like a business in a box, and it comes with a product or service, and a plan. A franchise also has a 75% greater success rate than a business started from scratch. Buying a franchise can help dramatically reduce risk and increase your chances of success. Of course, a franchise has pros and cons to consider, so do your research before buying into a franchise.

There is an important distinction between owning a business and being self-employed. Being self-employed is like a business because it gives you some freedoms apart from a normal job. Those freedoms can mean you are able to set your own hours and control your own pricing. However, being self-employed also has limits. For example, if you are self-employed and you get sick or take a vacation, nobody is doing your job. It means you're not earning any income unless you are actually working. In some ways this is worse than a regular job which might offer sick time or paid vacation time. To me, being self-employed actually means you own a job, not a business. A business is different because it continues to produce even when you're not there. A business has a team of people who continue the production while you are away either on vacation or pursuing some other purpose. It takes time and effort to grow a business to this point.

Today I own a real estate company. My company manages several hundred rental properties which produce consistent monthly income for both the company and the many property owners we serve. The real estate company also facilitates transactions for home buyers, sellers, and real estate investors. Today, the income earned from my company provides revenue even when I am not working. But it was not always this way. Before my company became a business, it started as just a job. Yes, I owned the job, but it was still a job I had to work. If I did not work, I did not get paid. So, I worked until there was enough business for me to hire help. Then we worked on it together until we could hire more help. Today I have a large team of people who support each other and keep the business working even if one of us is not there. The best part of my business is having my daughter involved. She has plans to take ownership some day and to pass it on to her kids. My company is a generational plan to leave a legacy for my children's children.

You may be thinking you don't want to own a business, and that's fine. However, if you love your job and have no intention of leaving it, you are still in business. This may sound strange, but to be the most effective in your job, you should start thinking of yourself as a corporation—a corporation of one. As the president and CEO of your corporation, your primary responsibility is to make sure your clients are happy with your product or service. If you are an employee, then your client is your employer. When you think about it, happy clients pay more for good service, but they change companies for bad service. Your job as president and CEO of your corporation/job is to assure the happiness of your client/employer. Your attitude will gain favor on the job and lead to promotions and raises and success for those around you.

It was the attitude of a servant which got Joseph promoted from his place in prison to his partnership with Pharaoh (Genesis 41). In today's economy, we need more Josephs, who will serve their employers and gain the favor and trust necessary to rise to positions of leadership within an enterprise. This is a very important part of God's plan for increase. Even if you're miserable at your current job, submit yourself to it. Allow God to prosper you in the place you're currently planted and trust Him to promote you to a better position. God will do it for you, just like He did it for Joseph. If you submit and serve the very best you can in your current circumstance, God will bring you success.

It is my opinion that the greatest witness I can be is a servant to those around me. I show Jesus Christ to my colleagues and clients by serving them and doing business with integrity. Consider this, Jesus first invited the disciples to join Him in His walk of life, before he asked them to believe in Him. It was then only after they had walked with Him for a while, that they finally started to believe in Him. Following His example, you can show those around you who Jesus is in your life by simply walking with them. In work or business, you walk with someone by simply serving them with your particular product or service. Simply put, you are called to serve in your business or workplace in such a manner that people see the love and character of Jesus in you.

Joseph was promoted because of his attitude of service. He served God by serving the people around him. In doing so, he gave honor to God, and God honored him through promotions, saving many nations. The Lord could very well use you to save a nation in the future. Start today by being a servant and honoring God at your business or place of work. By doing so, you will give God the opportunity to promote you and give you an increase in both pay and influence.

The greatest portion of your life is spent in your workplace, making it your greatest sphere of influence. You can see this principle demonstrated by Paul in Acts 18. As the chapter opens, Paul has left Athens and is headed to Corinth, where he met Aquila and his wife, Priscilla. He joined them in ministry and went into business with them. As a result of those relationships, a strong and thriving community became a part of the growing church (Acts 18:3). This principle shows the similar nature of business and ministry. Both are positions of service, both provide needs to the community, and both will grow and flourish through serving. A business, as well as a ministry, must provide valuable goods or services for its community to continue to exist.

They were glad to do this because they feel they owe a real debt to them. Since the Gentiles received the spiritual blessings of the Good News from the believers in Jerusalem, they feel the least they can do in return is to help them financially.
Romans 15:27

It is because of this service to the community, I feel everyone should be involved in business at some level. Whether it means serving your current employer to help him or her succeed, or you are moving toward the dream of owning a business. Even if you feel called to full-time ministry, you should still look at your ministry like a business that dutifully serves the community. In doing so, you will position yourself to operate more efficiently and make a greater impact on your community. Business also provides for personal gain. One of my early teachers explained some things to me like this. *If you want to get more money, then you'd better get good at dealing with people, because in today's society people show their appreciation toward you with their money.* Nowhere is this more clearly demonstrated than in business.

The next strategy for building wealth is investing. This is one of the most popular financial strategies and one of the easiest to enter. If you happen to have a retirement account then you probably already own stocks, bonds, or mutual funds within that retirement account. This can be a great way to grow long term wealth and increase financial security. It is the most common strategy used to build a retirement fund. But have you considered what you're investing in when you buy a stock, a bond, or a mutual fund? Chances are when you made the investment you made a quick look at some analyst's projected rate of return and decided to try a few shares. This is the investment strategy for many people, and it can occasionally yield moderate returns.

Since the goal is actually greater than moderate returns, you want to enter the world of investing with multiplication in mind. God is a God who multiplies, and it is His desire to give you the Kingdom. As good stewards over the resources God gives, you have a responsibility to gain knowledge through research and seek wisdom through prayer. It may help to think of your investment like this. When you buy stock in a company, you are actually loaning your money to the company. You have a responsibility to make sure the company is financially sound and able to repay the loan you are making. This likely puts a different spin on buying stocks than you've heard before, but it is a simple and accurate definition. Using this mindset, you can establish wise criteria to invest in a company.

One of the first things to research before you loan money to a company is their core values. Ask the question, does this company's core values line up with biblical principles? If they do not, you should not put Kingdom money into it. However, if the core values do align with God's Kingdom principles, you can look deeper into whether the company is a solid financial investment. The next thing I am looking for is the amount of debt-to-income ratio of the company. I would like to see that the company has its debts under control, and if it has a history of strong income, enabling it to both pay its debts and make a profit. To understand this requires knowing how to read a financial report. If you're interested, I would recommend a book appropriately titled, *How To Read a Financial Report*, by John A. Tracy.

There are many things to be considered when it comes to selecting stocks, bonds, or funds. Far too many for me to list within these pages. If you're interested in this type of savings approach, I recommend you do some research and educate yourself. The investment you make in this education is an investment in yourself. I would classify it as part of your 10-10-70-10 plan, the final 10% where you sharpen your ax.

The last of these three strategies is my favorite. The third wealth building strategy is investing in real estate. Real estate has created more millionaires than any other investment vehicle ever. When you invest in real estate you are buying an asset which can produce income while at the same time gaining in value through appreciation. The strategy of investing in real estate combines the benefits of owning a business with the benefits of owning an investment into a super wealth producing strategy.

When you buy a piece of real estate and convert it into a rental property you are performing a valuable service for your community. This service meets one of the three basic needs we as human beings have in life—food, clothing, and shelter. When you invest in real estate you are providing shelter for other families. In exchange for shelter they pay you money in the form of rent. If you buy a rental property with a mortgage loan, then the rents from your tenants are working to pay off the loan for you. This is a beautiful application of compounded interest that can bring exponential growth to your financial portfolio.

As an example, let's say you bought a rental property for $100,000, and put $20,000 down then took out a loan for $80,000 to complete the purchase. With mortgage rates at the time of this writing, the total payment including principal, interest, taxes, and insurance would be around $700 per month. If you then rented the house for $1,000 per month you would have a positive income of $300 per month, or $3,600 per year, which equates to an 18% cash on cash return on your investment. We can find the return by taking the amount of positive annual income and dividing it by the amount of cash invested. So, $3,600 per year divided by a $20,000 down payment equals an 18% return. This alone is a great return, but with a rental property there is even more. Additionally, you would also have your tenant going to work every day and making payments toward the remaining $80,000 loan for the property. If you have a tenant living there long enough, they will pay the house off for you and put cash in your pocket every month as they do so.

Now let's say you hold the house for the entire 30 years it takes to pay off the mortgage. If nothing changed during those 30 years, you would have received the benefit of $300 positive income every month, which over 30 years would total $108,000. Plus, you would have had your tenant pay off your original $80,000 mortgage, making the amount of cash you received on your initial $20,000 investment to be a total of $188,000. Of course, we must also consider the appreciation of the house—the asset you bought. According to the average appreciation rate over the last 100 years on real estate at 6.2% per year, the home value would be at more than $607,000.

If you add all this up, the total return on your $20,000 investment is more than $715,000. You could say there was a significant return on an investment and a fair demonstration of the power of leveraging a small amount into a large return. Now imagine you do the same thing just four or five times during your lifetime. You would leave a lasting legacy of wealth for your children which could continue to grow for their children and beyond. This is why I love Real Estate.

This was a very basic example, not considering other aspects of owning a piece of rental property. This example did not consider maintenance cost during those 30 years, nor the rents increasing, or the valuable tax benefits which come with rental properties. This was merely a basic example of the power of investing in real estate. It is a great combination of business and investing which can yield large returns on small investments with a minimum amount of labor.

In Luke 19:13 Jesus tells a parable of the Mina where He hands out portions of money to His servants then commands them to *use this to earn more money until I get back.* You can do this with any of the three strategies above, or you can mix them together for accelerated gains. But no matter which strategy you choose to employ, approach it with expectation and understanding. Your increase will come in finance and influence, which is the desire of God for all of His children. Building your financial portfolio is part of your responsibility to steward your finances, and a big part of stewardship is considering the proper structure for your business or portfolio holdings. Whether you plan to start a small, home-based business, build a large corporation, or invest in income streams like rental property, you need to establish a solid foundation in the Word and prayer.

With so many options to consider, I recommend prayer before planting seed in **any** field. When you submit your plans to God, He will show you the best fields to plant in. In Genesis 26 the chapter opens by saying there was a famine in the land where God told Isaac to plant. It appears from reading this passage, Isaac had planned to move where he thought he would find greener pastures. God told him not to go to Egypt, but to stay in the land and plant his seed. In verse 12, Isaac obeyed God and in spite of the famine he reaped a crop of one hundredfold. Isaac's increase was manifest because he submitted his plans to God, and then obeyed. It is always God's plan for you to increase. Whatever plans you submit to Him will be directed toward the proper actions to bring about your increase.

I could continue on with business opportunities, or strategies for additional income streams, but it should be included in a different book. This book is about introducing you to God's plan for increasing your finances. I recommend you ask Him to show you the investment plans He has for you. In the meantime, your job is to be a good steward of the resources He has entrusted to you.

This chapter was a quick overview of strategies available to you. What I have been able to give you here is only an introduction to the process of cultivating and caring for your fields. My intention was to wake you up to strategies which can build wealth. As you start to research and employ some of these strategies, you will enjoy watching your savings, your business, and your investments grow. As these fields develop, you will find yourself with even more seed available. You will have extra seed to plant even more crops and develop even more fields of income to provide for you and the community around you.

It is through this increase you will achieve greater influence in your community and a greater reach for the Kingdom of God. Welcome to the Kingdom Economy.

Chapter 13

Kingdom Economy in Action

So he called ten of his servants, delivered to them ten minas, and said to them, 'Do business till I come. Luke 19:13 NKJV

There is no actual Hebrew word for businessman. The word most often used is a word which literally means *man of faith*. I find this to be a very accurate translation of what it is to do business. It takes a great amount of faith to invest in something at one price and believe you can sell it for a higher price. That is the picture of faith in action.

Jesus' command for us to *do business until He comes* is a command which requires us to step out in faith. This is the same kind of faith Isaac displayed in Genesis 26 when he planted seed during a time of famine. We are called to operate in the same kind of faith by planting seed to bring an increase. This kind of faith requires a measure of risk, without which there would be no reward.

Yes, the king replied, and to those who use well what they are given, even more will be given. But from those who do nothing, even what little they have will be taken away. Luke 19:26

In Luke 19 Jesus is looking for people who will multiply their money. No matter what your goal is in life, money is necessary to achieve it. Money helps to influence communities for righteousness, spread the gospel, feed the homeless, and to care for the poor and the widows. Money is what you use to buy the things you need, whether for your life or the work of the ministry. It stands to reason the more money God can put into the hands of His people, the more effective they will be at building His Kingdom. This was the goal Jesus had in mind when He set out in search of those who would multiply the resources He entrusted to them.

Zacchaeus was one of the men Jesus was looking for, and his story is in Luke 19:1–9. He was a chief tax collector, making it safe to assume he was not popular in the community. He is described as being very rich and someone who wanted to see Jesus. As the story goes, Jesus was coming to town when a large group of people were crowding the streets to see Him. Zacchaeus was too short to see over the crowds, so he climbed a tree to get a better look at the master. Jesus noticed Zacchaeus and called out to him.

When Jesus came by, he looked up at Zacchaeus and called him by name. "Zacchaeus!" he said. "Quick, come down! I must be a guest in your home today. Luke 19:5

Jesus' comment caused the crowd to gasp. They simply could not understand why Jesus would take the time to notice Zacchaeus, let alone stay with him. But Jesus not only requested to stay at his house, He said he *must* stay at his house. Zacchaeus was a rich man Jesus sought out. Today Jesus is still seeking out wealthy people. He wants you to attract the lost, influence your community, and build the Kingdom. From this passage, it is clear Jesus was not looking for Zacchaeus simply because of his money. Jesus ignited honesty and integrity within Zacchaeus transforming him from a despised member of society to a man who could influence his community. Verse 10 confirms Jesus' mission to seek and save the lost. He wants to see businesspeople of high integrity resourcing and furthering the Kingdom.

Meanwhile, Zacchaeus stood before the Lord and said, "I will give half my wealth to the poor, Lord, and if I have cheated people on their taxes, I will give them back four times as much!" Jesus responded, "Salvation has come to this home today, for this man has shown himself to be a true son of Abraham. For the Son of Man came to seek and save those who are lost. Luke 19:8-10

In response to the crowd's disgust over Jesus socializing with sinners, Jesus Himself announced He came to restore what was lost! He continues addressing issues outside the traditional frame of reference by telling a parable dealing with finances.

The crowd was listening to everything Jesus said. And because he was nearing Jerusalem, he told them a story to correct the impression that the Kingdom of God would begin right away. He said, "A nobleman was called away to a distant empire to be crowned king and then return. Before he left, he called together ten of his servants and divided among them ten pounds of silver, saying, 'Invest this for me while I am gone. Luke 19:11-13

Jesus' encounter with Zacchaeus began with a rich man, then He continued dealing with the people's hearts through a parable addressing finances. Jesus was showing the Kingdom of God very definitely includes God's Kingdom Economy. In the above parable, a nobleman is leaving for a distant empire to be crowned king. One interpretation places Jesus as the nobleman, who was walking the Earth, but would be going to Heaven to receive His own crown. The command He gave His servants was, *Invest this for me while I am gone* or another translation states, *do business until He returns*. The same command is still in effect today. I want to point out in the next verse 14, it says the citizens of the land hated him. Jesus was entrusting resources to His servants and asking them to do business in a hostile environment.

Today, society is very much a hostile environment, where the economy is dominated by the enemy's plans and purposes. The economy of this world is built on the principle of ownership and revolves around the buying and selling of goods. The economy Jesus came to restore is an economy based on stewardship. It is built on the principles of giving and receiving. Clearly these economies operate opposite each other. When you choose to live by God's Kingdom Economy, you will be operating in a world which is hostile to believers. It was the wise servants who understood how to operate in a hostile economy and were able to do business and multiply the resources their master entrusted to them. See Luke 19:16–19.

Operating in a hostile environment starts with stewardship. This book contains a simple plan, but the plan is only a guide and is not to be taken as law. Whether you follow the 10-10-70-10 plan or find a variation which works for you, begin to control your finances and start filling your silo with seed to sow into your fields. Imagine the freedom you will feel as your savings account starts to grow due to your new, healthy relationship with money. A healthy relationship which puts you in charge, telling your dollars what to do, then watching them do it. Only through effective stewardship can you fill your silo and become the multiplier God intends you to be. A silo full of seed gives you the freedom to be an investor, fulfilling the great commandment of our Lord to do business until He comes.

The phrase, *do business* or *invest,* means to carry on the business of a banker or a trader. Both of those professions result in the multiplication of financial resources. A trader is one who buys and sells goods. He will buy his goods at a price which allows him to sell them for a higher price to realize a profit or increase. A banker is one who trades money, often through the process of investing. The increase which comes through the process of investing is generally referred to as interest, which is also increase! God intends for you to increase in order to build His house and bring glory to His Kingdom.

Increase comes easier when you reach for it with righteous intentions. It can be elusive when the motivation for increase is greed, spurred on by the spirit of mammon. But you are now wise to those strategies, being able to recognize an evil influence and steer free of its traps. When you are pursuing money through a healthy relationship, you will glorify God and be able to reach beyond the limitations of the world's economy. You will be able to tap into the fruit of increase God will supply to fulfill your purpose and destiny.

Building the Kingdom is the ultimate goal. It takes money to build the Kingdom, which is why God prospers you and brings increase to your resources. God intends for businesspeople to be multipliers who use their resources to build His Kingdom. This is not a new concept. This is how the Kingdom was designed from the start, evidenced throughout biblical history. God often used anointed businesspeople to help build His Kingdom.

Start with Abraham, the father of our Faith. Abram's father was a merchant, a businessman, so it is logical to think Abram knew business. It is no surprise then to read how God prospered Abraham throughout his life with business dealings. The Bible speaks of Abraham as a man made very wealthy in livestock, and in silver and gold, which are commodities gained by trading. The same kind of trading Jesus has called you to participate in.

There is another example in the building of the Tabernacle of Moses. You can read the story in Exodus 35. This passage shows how the first tabernacle was designed and built, but I want to focus on **who** God used to build it.

Then the Lord said to Moses, "Look, I have specifically chosen Bezalel son of Uri, grandson of Hur, of the tribe of Judah. I have filled him with the Spirit of God, giving him great wisdom, ability, and expertise in all kinds of crafts. He is a master craftsman, expert in working with gold, silver, and bronze. He is skilled in engraving and mounting gemstones and in carving wood. He is a master at every craft!
Exodus 31:1-5

It is significant to note the very first person recorded in the Bible as being filled with the Spirit was Bezalel, an anointed man from the marketplace. Today God is calling you to be an anointed businessperson who comes from the marketplace bearing the increase God has blessed you with to help build His Kingdom, just as Bezalel did. If you're like me, you have dreamed of doing your part to help build the Kingdom of God. The Scriptures say, preach the good news and set people free which is certainly part of building the Kingdom. But everyone is not called to be a pastor or a full-time minister. In fact, out of the 12 tribes, only one was called to the priestly duties, while the other 11 were called to the marketplace to bring multiplication. As your money grows through trading and investing, you can be like Bezalel, anointed from the marketplace, who contributes your talents, and resources to help build God's Kingdom.

As your finances increase, your influence will also increase. Soon you will be asked to step in and do the things you've only dreamed of. Your grand dreams, the desires of your heart are from the Lord. As your influence grows, so will your ability to fulfill the dreams and purposes God has placed in your heart. Your level of creativity will also increase, and soon new visions, new dreams, and new ways of doing things will come to you. All this increase will bring new revelations and new strategies to employ as you do your part to build the Kingdom.

This is further symbolized in the building of Solomon's Temple—the greatest temple of its time—built when the nation of Israel was at its highest point of prosperity. This temple was also built with the help of an anointed businessperson, Huram from Tyre. His name means noble born and he was from a wealthy nation of merchants who prospered through trading.

I am sending you a master craftsman named Huram-abi, who is extremely talented. His mother is from the tribe of Dan in Israel, and his father is from Tyre. He is skillful at making things from gold, silver, bronze, and iron, and he also works with stone and wood. He can work with purple, blue, and scarlet cloth and fine linen. He is also an engraver and can follow any design given to him. He will work with your craftsmen and those appointed by my lord David, your father.
2 Chronicles 2:13-14

Huram was empowered by God to help build Solomon's temple, and he brought his skill into the design and construction. He gained a unique understanding through his extensive knowledge of business and ministry and how they were meant to work together. Huram's mother was an Israelite, and his father was from Tyre. As a child of two different cultures, Huram learned the ways of God **and** the ways of business. God lifted him to a position of influence because of the unique wisdom and insight he possessed. Huram used every gift God gave him in the building of the temple of Solomon. On a practical level, Huram saw the need for anointed businesspeople to work jointly in the whole endeavor.

Huram designed and built the two main pillars which stood and supported the entrance—the porch or portico—to Solomon's Temple.

Huram set the pillars at the entrance of the Temple, one toward the south and one toward the north. He named the one on the south Jakin, and the one on the north Boaz. 1 Kings 7:21

Each of the two pillars which stood at the entrance of Solomon's temple had a name, delineating purpose and operation of the temple. Those same distinctions are applicable today. The first pillar was named Jakin, meaning *He will establish*. Jakin was at one time the head of one of the priestly lines who ministered over Israel. This pillar indicates the operation of the temple is to establish a ministry to God and to the people. As a living temple of the Holy Spirit, part of your purpose and operation is to worship God and minister His love to those in and around your community.

The second pillar was named Boaz, meaning *in Him is strength*. Boaz was the vitally important kinsman redeemer in the book of Ruth. He was a businessman and a community leader. He not only controlled great wealth, but he used it to serve his community. This pillar states the operation of the temple is to lead and to influence through the strength of God. Again, as a living temple of the Holy Spirit, you have the responsibility to lead and influence your community allowing His Kingdom to come and His will to be done.

When considered together, these two pillars give a complete image of how you are meant to operate in your community today. Combining the ministering work of a priest with the redeeming work of a businessperson through the established strength of the Lord, will bring impact for the Kingdom. When these two pillars come together in action, the Body of Christ has its greatest impact on society.

Take a quick look at the story of Ruth. Ruth and her mother-in-law Naomi were drawn back to Israel during a time of famine because they heard there was bread in the land. This bread was not what is given out on Sunday morning communion. It was the kind of bread which sustains life. and can only be acquired through economic activity. Boaz was a leader in his community because of his economic activity. He had fields of grain which provided jobs for workers and food to be sold by the merchants in the marketplace. Boaz also sat on the council and conferred with leaders and priests of his day. As part of this group, Boaz was not only inspired by the priests, but he carried their word into his place of business. He recognized the hand of God as the source of his prosperity. It was his prosperity which attracted Ruth and her mother-in-law Naomi to his fields. And it was his prosperity that led to their salvation. Boaz recognized this and gave the Lord glory for allowing him to be part of the wonderful redeeming work in this story.

May the Lord, the God of Israel, under whose wings you have come to take refuge, reward you fully for what you have done.
Ruth 2:12

If it were not for the influence Boaz had in the marketplace, Ruth may not have been saved and this story may never have been written.

It's not just biblical stories illustrating the importance of marketplace influence. There are more modern age examples like the great missionary work of the Moravians. This group of believers are known for beginning a 100-year prayer movement and for sending missionaries throughout the known world. Their prayer movement was a ministry activity which ultimately launched an economic outreach. The Moravians were so moved to touch the world around them, that they launched a plan to open trading outposts in locations around the world. Those trading outposts were not only for economic increase, they were also strategically placed in lands they had prayed over and targeted to reach the lost. It was through the economic activity of their trading outposts the Moravian missionaries ministered to the communities. They recognized the need to combine both the work of the ministry and the work of the businessperson to more effectively reach the world around them.

Today, the calling falls on you. It is now your responsibility to prosper in order to reach into the fields and attract a great harvest. It is encouraging to see the church is changing in this direction. God is moving into the marketplace. He is calling people like you to prosper and increase through business and trade to provide the resources needed to build His Kingdom. With this new understanding you can begin to see God's economy as a healthy balance of spirit-led people ministering to community needs through economic activity. It is through this economic activity we are able to multiply the resources to attract the lost, influence communities, and build the Kingdom.

As builders of His Kingdom, be prepared to minister to the economic needs of the community around you. Through business and economic activity in the marketplace, you will be able to reach souls who may never set foot in a church. I've seen this in my own business. Several years ago, armed with this revelation, I approached a pastor friend of mine about forming a partnership and opening a business to minister to people in need. My friend's ministry focused on feeding the homeless community in downtown Orlando. Together we crafted a plan to minister to these homeless people through economic opportunities—we started a home remodeling company. We would focus on distressed properties being purchased by local investors and complete the rehab and renovation process by hiring from the homeless community. With this new mix of business and ministry we were not only restoring homes, we were also restoring lives.

At first, we only hired a few people. But the project quickly grew to several crews working in stages on multiple properties across the city. Our process was focused mainly on the lives of the men and women we employed. We would meet each morning at a warehouse and spend the first hour of the day sharing and talking over their needs, their perceptions, their ideas, and their dreams. Then we would pray corporately and for each one individually as needed. We also incorporated counseling for those who needed additional help beyond what we could give on the job. In addition, we had legal counselors available to help them settle any outstanding legal issues. Some of them had extensive collections or even warrants for outstanding citations which needed to be cleared up.

The day we hired each person we took them off the streets and put them into a house where we had set up rooms for each one to rent. The rooms were furnished with a clean bed and clean sheets and a common area kitchen and dining area where they could fellowship with other people who were on the same journey. Acting as trustees, we set up financial counseling and opened bank accounts in their name as many could not qualify to get a bank account on their own. We taught them financial stewardship, how to give, how to pay themselves through savings, and how to invest in themselves using the 10-10-70-10 plan. After six months, the average person had a little over $1000 in his savings account and was able to take over the management of their bank account on their own.

Not all the men and women who came to work with us grew and prospered. Sadly, there were those who chose to return to their homeless, drug-filled lifestyle. But there were also those who grabbed hold of the change and began to prosper. We had several who outgrew what we could offer them as a small company and went to work with some of our partner corporations on bigger projects. Some were even hired on high end projects with Disney and Universal Studios. Our efforts of combining business and ministry made a major impact and changed lives. We were able to double and triple the impact of the ministry sharing free food with them downtown. When business and ministry come together, the results can be measured exponentially.

I see this in my current business as well. I am not hiring homeless people today, but people who have skills for a job regardless of their beliefs. In one case I hired a guy named Joe, who was a very gruff individual. His vocabulary consisted of very few words, and he seemed to have one particular favorite word that he used very creatively in almost every sentence. His favorite word being *the F word.* Joe had a sordid history. He had spent time in a prison, he had committed countless acts of violence, and was an active member of a very large motorcycle gang known to be involved in criminal activity. Joe often told me he did not believe there was a God and if there was one, God would have nothing to do with him.

I admit I had to be selective about which jobs I gave to Joe, mostly based on the people he would need to interact with. But in spite of everything in Joe's past, I found him honest and skillful in the jobs I gave him. Joe did many jobs for me over a span of about three years. He gave me a good price, and he stood behind his work. He did a good job, which prompted me to give him more projects, and if there was a problem with his work, he would always fix it. In the time I knew Joe, we became friends. He would often randomly text me, just to say hi or share some news. He even invited me to come to his exclusive brotherhood clubhouse. I knew it was a special thing because he considered the biker club to be his family. He demonstrated the love he had for this family in everything he said and did. I know the invitation was a big deal to him, and I didn't take it lightly. I honored his request and accepted his invitation.

When I arrived at his clubhouse there were several leather-clad bikers acting as guards at the gate. They questioned who we were and why we were there. I let them know Joe had invited me and it turned out he had already let them know I was coming. They escorted us (my wife and I) into a run-down, dark building which had been adopted as their clubhouse. There were posters and paraphernalia hanging on the wall, none fit for display in a Christian household. There was an old bar made of plywood, standing on a painted concrete floor with some scattered stools and a smattering of chairs. It was essentially an old, smoke-filled shack—not the kind of place I would hang out on a Friday night. But to Joe, this was like home, and it meant so much to him when I accepted his invitation to visit. Out of honor for my relationship with Joe, we spent a few hours hanging out at the clubhouse and meeting some of his closest friends.

It was sometime later, on a random Wednesday afternoon, when Joe walked into my office and asked to talk with me. I'll admit it was not a good time to see him as I was busy with other things. Also, Joe generally smelled like an old, never-cleaned ashtray and the smell lingered in my office for hours after he left. But this day was different. Joe had a look on his face I had never seen before. The look was a cry for help, and he asked to talk to me privately. He looked at me sincerely, told me I was the most pious guy he knew and asked if I would pray for him. I have to admit I was shocked. Here was a guy who for years had denied God existed, and now he was asking me to pray with him. It was an invitation I eagerly accepted.

I will never forget that day. I had prayed for Joe since I had known him, but I never actually thought the day would come when he would surrender. Praise God he did, and I finished the day knowing the Holy Spirit had touched a lost soul. Someone who had been touched through the reach of a business God had blessed me with. The day changed not only my life, but it changed Joe for eternity. It was only three days later when I realized how significant Joe's visit had been. Three days after Joe visited me at my office, he was killed in a motorcycle accident. In the prayer he and I shared, God was reaching out, giving Joe one last chance for salvation. Graciously, through our prayer together he was joined with Jesus for eternity. I know the reason I had the opportunity to pray with Joe was the trust I had built with him during the years of doing business. He would likely never have stepped into a church and asked for salvation, but he came to my business because he needed a job.

It was the same economic need which drove Naomi and Ruth into the fields of Boaz. It's the same economic need which draws countless souls into the Kingdom. Today the call falls on you. It is up to you to expand His Kingdom. And it is through the combined forces of ministry and economic activity that His Kingdom will be built.

This call also comes with a warning. A warning to practice the principles of stewarding your money. A warning to take care you are not consumed with pride and deceived by your own wealth. A warning to experience the increase and prosperity of God's blessing to further His Kingdom. The warning is contained in the words of Moses in Deuteronomy 8:18. **Do not forget it is God who gives the power to get wealth.** Today this warning is just as important as it was all those years ago. It is God who gives wealth, and the purpose of your wealth is to build the Kingdom of God.

His calling comes with a challenge only you can answer. A challenge to stand up and effectively steward the resources God has given you. When you honor Him with your stewardship, He can honor you by bringing increase. Imagine how different your life will be by applying these spiritual principles and disciplines to your finances. When you answer God's call to be a multiplier, He can increase your resources and give you influence in your community.

As you continue to recognize the influence of the spirit of mammon, you can keep it from negatively impacting your life and finances. You can also expose its influence over others and minister freedom to them. Your influence can result in more effective programs and ministries in your community. You could know the joy of supporting and giving them the ability to flourish. You could know the joys of being a giver and seeing your resources bear amazing fruit.

I will finish by sharing one final thought. Imagine money is like the snowfall on top of a mountain. Each year a new supply of snow falls and although it slowly melts through the summer, it's never completely gone, but continues to pile higher each winter. The snow is a picture of a never-ending supply, and money is actually a never-ending supply when God is involved. Truly, a never-ending supply. The supply which eventually comes to you depends on how obedient you are with your portion.

If you feel the supply (snow melt) is limited and you need to build a dam to capture enough to sustain yourself. Very quickly you will find the flow is cut off and you will have nothing more to give. But if you start digging irrigation ditches to supply the fields around you, the snow melt will fill your reservoir and nourish the other fields as well. You will be cared for and you will care for many others. Your money will feed more than your family. There will be enough for all those around you. Never forget, money is called currency because it flows like the current of a river coming from the ice pack on a distant mountain top. Every irrigation ditch you dig to water the fields around you only serves to increase the flow coming to you.

As you apply these spiritual principles and disciplines in your life, you will experience new freedoms which may have seemed elusive before. You will find a new joy in giving as an ability to support good works is released over you. There will be new joy in your relationships and in your marriage as the worries over money dissipate and God's favor overcomes you. As your finances grow, your influence will grow in your home, your job or business and your church and community. You are now an influencer for the Kingdom and free to do all the Lord has placed in your heart to do.

So step into the river of increase God has for you and begin to live out the dreams and purposes He's given you. With your increase you will be more empowered than ever to cast out the darkness that surrounds your community, and set the captives free from their bondage, and bear much fruit as your sphere of influence, and the Kingdom of God grows around you. God wants to prosper you, He wants to grant you riches to fulfill the destiny He has placed in your heart. While it is true you cannot serve God and money, you can serve God with your money.

Father, I pray that these truths would pierce my heart and change me forever, that money would forever be the slave that you have meant it to be, in that you will show me how to use it as a beacon and a light that brings hope to the people whose lives you've called me to touch. Father, I ask that you would continue to pour out more truths to teach me how to live in your economy and bring hope that ministers to the material needs of the community that you've called me to live in.

Amen

Declaration

One Final word. There is power in declaration. I recommend you make a declaration as soon as you are ready to see growth and change in your life. I have provided a sample declaration below. This promise to the Lord, is a contract with yourself as a covenant seal to empower you to receive the blessings the Lord has for you. Share your declaration with your family and hold it before the Lord in prayer. Keep it in a place to remind you of a covenant empowering you to receive all the blessings God has for you.

THE DECLARATION OF FINANCIAL INDEPENDENCE

I solemnly resolve before The Lord God, My Family, and Friends to commit with all steadfastness and purposefulness to follow this creed in order to Eliminate My Debts, Increase My Income, and Build True Wealth for God, My Family, and My Community. I hereby declare:

- To handle my finances according to God's word by putting the Almighty God first in my life honoring him first with my tithe and offerings.
  "Honor the Lord with your wealth, with the first fruits of all your crops; then your barns will be filled to overflowing, and your vats will brim over with new wine." Proverbs 3: 9 & 10

- To take full responsibility of myself, my spouse, and my children by committing to limit my spending and save a portion of my income.
  "A good man leaves an inheritance for his children's children..." Proverbs 13:22

- To live a meek and margined lifestyle and no longer over spend my time or the time of my spouse and/or my children and my income.
  "Blessed are the meek for they shall inherit the earth." Matthew 5:5

- To consecrate myself and my house from all forms of Idolatry that anger God and erode my relationship with Him and my family keeping me trapped in debt.
  "I am the Lord your God; consecrate yourself and be holy, because I am holy. Do not make yourself unclean by anything that moves on the Earth. I am the Lord who brought you up out of slavery to be your God; therefore be holy, because I am holy." Leviticus 11:44 & 45

- To allow myself to dream and speak those dreams that God has placed in my heart in order to excite and motivate myself daily staying steadfast and committed to paying off my debts, freeing myself from man's slavery, and empowering myself to fulfill the purpose God has called me to.

  "May he give you the desire of your heart and make all your plans succeed." Psalms 20:4

  "Delight yourself in the Lord for he gives you the desires of your heart." Psalms 37: 4

- To diligently believe and expect new opportunities, promotions, and increase as I follow God's plan for my life and my finances.
  "Whoever can be trusted with little can also be trusted with much..." Luke 16:10

____

Signature *Date*

____________________ ____________________

Witness Signature *Date* *Witness Signature* *Date*

If you prefer, you can also download a copy of this declaration from my web site.

www.troylpeterson.com/declaration

www.ingramcontent.com/pod-product-compliance
Lightning Source LLC
La Vergne TN
LVHW020717110826
845149LV00012B/2296

9798989968800